GLIDING
WITH RADIO CONTROL

A BEGINNER'S GUIDE TO
BUILDING AND FLYING MODEL SAILPLANES

MARTIN SIMONS

Nexus Special Interests

Nexus Special Interests Ltd
Nexus House
Azalea Drive
Swanley
Kent BR8 8HU
England

First published in the USA 1994

This edition first published by Nexus Special Interests Ltd., 1998

ISBN 1-85486-173-5

Typeset by Kate Williams, Swansea.
Printed and bound in Great Britain by Biddles Ltd., Guildford & King's Lynn

CONTENTS

ABOUT THIS BOOK   iv

FOREWORD   vi

1   GETTING HELP   1

2   COSTS: THE RADIO EQUIPMENT   3

3   COSTS: THE FIRST GLIDER   6

4   FIELD EQUIPMENT   10

5   THE GLIDER: LAYOUT AND STRUCTURE   16

6   SOME FINER POINTS OF DESIGN   23

7   THE RADIO CONTROL GEAR   29

8   BUILDING THE MODEL   36

9   FITTING THE RADIO INTO THE MODEL   47

10 BALANCING THE MODEL   58

11 HOW THE GLIDER FLIES   62

12 HOW THE GLIDER CONTROLS WORK   69

13 LEARNING TO FLY   75

14 LAUNCHING   92

15 LANDING   95

16 SOARING   100

17 WHAT NEXT?   111

APPENDIX 1   FURTHER READING   117

APPENDIX 2   GLOSSARY   119

ABOUT THIS BOOK

This book is intended for the absolute beginner in the building and flying of radio controlled gliders. No previous knowledge or experience of the sport is assumed.

The first important suggestion, repeated here, is that the beginner should seek advice before, rather than after, spending money on equipment or struggling with a model that may be unsuitable. Starting off is not quite as easy as it may seem although, with some help, the learning process is not long. The guidance of an experienced instructor and membership of a recognised model flying club is desirable. Relatives and friends giving presents to young people should take special note of this.

Yet there is enough in this text to enable anyone who is unable to find an instructor to make a beginning without too many frustrating errors.

You are taken slowly through all the important steps from an outline of the likely initial costs, the choice of a first model and the radio control gear, through launching methods and equipment onwards to the earliest flights, circuit planning and landing. The facts and ideas are explained simply but accurately. There is a glossary, giving the meaning of special words and phrases – nothing is taken for granted.

Finally there is some valuable advice about more advanced manoeuvres and simple aerobat-ics, leading to the thrilling experience of hill and thermal soaring. A last short section outlines the possibilities for further enjoyment, including competition and task flying, scale sailplanes, and other kinds of radio controlled aviation.

I can still recall the feeling of total confusion that almost overwhelmed me when, as a boy, I opened my very first model aeroplane kit. There was an exciting picture on the box. Inside were some little sticks of balsa wood, a couple of flimsy sheets of the same material marked with puzzling shapes, a bit of wire, a small chunk of hardwood and an incomprehensible plan.

That model was never completed. Some kits offered on the market today are not much better, although they are bigger and cost more. They are capable of being made up into excellent models but inexperienced buyers, lacking guidance, tend to flounder. Many potentially good models are left unfinished. Mistakes of construction are often seen when beginners arrive hopefully at the flying field for their first lessons. Models are often seriously damaged on their very first outing.

People attracted by the fascination of model soaring may easily be discouraged by such sad experiences. In most cases, all they need is a few words of explanation at the start. This book contains these explanations.

It is not necessary to read the book strictly in the order of the chapters – some of you will wish to skip ahead to the sections on learning to fly, and may come back to the more theoretical material only later. It is, however, quite important for the beginner to have some clear ideas about how the model flies, what it is and is not able to do, and how the controls work.

A feature of the book is a series of photographs with explanatory captions, following through the building of a simple training sailplane from a kit, showing it being put together and finally successfully flown. The book ends with some suggestions about going on to further model flying.

I was born in England in 1930 and can hardly remember a time when I was not involved with model flying. I am also an experienced pilot of full-sized sailplanes, with the international Gold C badge and two diamonds. I have done about 1500 hours' total time soaring, with many kilometres of cross-country flying. I have written extensively about soaring flight in all its aspects and was for ten years the editor of *Australian Gliding*, the official journal of the Gliding Federation of Australia. I contribute articles to magazines in both the full-sized and model flying areas. One of my books, *Model Aircraft Aerodynamics* (published by Nexus Special Interests), is recognised as the standard English language text on the subject (it is also available in German translation). I design, build and fly my own model sailplanes regularly in South Australia, where I now live.

Martin Simons, Australia, 1998

FOREWORD

MODEL GLIDERS ARE FUN

Flying radio controlled gliders has a wide appeal. Glider flying is a fascinating sport, not merely a training for power flying. Dedicated glider fliers find soaring at least as interesting as flying with an engine – many model fliers do both.

Sailplanes, as they are often called, may be flown for long periods over flat ground to soar in thermals and over hills to gain height in winds blowing up the slopes. There are systems for gaining certificates of proficiency. Aerobatics and races are possible as well as duration, speed and distance tests. Club, state, national and international championships are organised. People of all kinds are to be found in the membership of a model glider flying group.

Gliders create no noise. Permission to operate them in public open spaces and parks, with proper safety precautions, is much easier to obtain than for engine-powered model aeroplanes.

Most radio controlled glider fliers build their own aircraft and some become designers, sketching, drawing and redrawing plans, building, flying and experimenting to create new sailplanes which, perhaps, will fly better than the older types.

There are some direct uses for the knowledge gained. The basic principles of flight are the same whatever the size of the aircraft, with engines or without. Full-sized aircraft prototypes are sometimes tested in radio controlled model form. Most people who fly model gliders, however, do it just for fun.

TRY IT!

People sometimes hesitate to try radio controlled gliding because they believe the costs are high, the skills needed too hard to learn, or the equipment unreliable, delicate and prone to damage. This book should help to remove the worst of these doubts. Modern radio control equipment is highly reliable and remarkably robust, requiring no electronic expertise to operate. The costs are not crippling. Models do get broken but can be repaired. The skills needed are developed by experience but to make a start, advice and a little practical instruction are required.

chapter one

GETTING HELP

It is possible to teach yourself to build and fly a radio controlled model glider but anyone learning alone is in for many disappointments and it takes time and determination to get over these. It can be done but is not recommended. This is true even if you have some experience of flying full-sized aeroplanes or sailplanes. Controlling a model in the air while standing on the ground, is different from and in some ways more difficult than being in the cockpit. I write from experience of both.

If you live far away from any possibility of assistance, this book may help in avoiding the worst difficulties, but can hardly replace personal instruction.

HELPING THE YOUNG BEGINNER

If you are a parent or have young relatives, a flying model kit with radio gear is a very exciting gift but any youngster will need help and encouragement with it. Progress will be quicker with a little instruction. Begin by making contact with someone who knows what the beginner will require before, rather than after, buying equipment.

A powered model, whether fitted with an electric motor or a small liquid-fuelled engine, is not the easiest way to start. Some department stores are too ready to sell these aircraft, which are sometimes labelled 'self-launching sailplanes', to beginners. They fly well in experienced hands but they are not very suitable for the complete novice. They are also more expensive than gliders.

If your heart is set on power flying most beginners' gliders can be modified fairly easily to take an engine, after the required flying skills have been learned. It is easy to convert from gliding to powered flying, but it is not easy to rebuild a smashed and costly powered model after a bad crash. Far too many young people are bitterly disappointed after such quite unnecessary experiences.

JOIN A CLUB

It is much better to tackle the early stages under guidance from an experienced person. Such people can be found in model flying clubs. Permission to use public or private land for model flying is often restricted to club members. There are other important reasons for joining a club, which will be mentioned later.

If there is no club within reach, there may be a model flier living somewhere nearby who will be delighted to teach another potential enthusiast. It takes only two people to form a club!

MODEL SHOPS

Failing immediate contact with an active club, a shop specialising in radio controlled flying model aircraft is a good place to make first inquiries. Shops involved in this trade are sure to have on display one or two gliders, kits to build them and suitable radio control equipment. On the staff there will usually be someone with direct experience of the kind needed to advise the novice glider flier. Staff in such a shop should at least know where a club can be found or know other people who fly model gliders.

The model shop proprietor knows that future customers come from satisfied and successful beginners, so it is very unlikely that bad advice, shoddy goods, or totally unsuitable equipment will be offered.

Articles helpful to beginners feature in model flying magazines, some of which are listed in Appendix 1.

TOYSHOPS AND DEPARTMENT STORES

Glider kits and radios are sold in general toyshops and the toy departments of large stores. The equipment is often just the same as that in the specialist model shops but the staff of the store are not likely to be able to give the detailed advice that is really needed in the early stages.

chapter two

COSTS:
THE RADIO EQUIPMENT

The chief item of expense is the radio. A simple, **two function** or **two channel** set of radio control equipment is not expensive. It will include a **transmitter**, a **receiver** for the model, two **servos** to drive the controls, a **switch** and all the necessary leads and connecting plugs. Such sets are advertised for around £40–£50.

Batteries will be required. If ordinary dry batteries are used these will often need replacement. A set with rechargeable batteries will cost more at first and will include a **charger**. More is said about this below.

A simple two channel transmitter. The control stick on the right is for the rudder and will move only from side to side. The left-hand stick is for the elevator and moves forward and back. The aerial is fully extended. The socket for the crystal on this set is at the bottom left side of the case, the on-off switch at the bottom right.

Two model sailplanes with rudder and elevator controls only. The nearer one is the same type as that which was built to illustrate this book but has transparent wing covering. The rear one is smaller and lighter but not, in fact, so easy to build and fly.

A two function set is capable of operating two controls on the glider, normally the **rudder** and the **elevator**, which is enough to start with, but the beginner will soon outgrow it.

It is possible to spend a lot of money on radio equipment but it is not often necessary. The lower transmitter in the picture is an inexpensive four function set, perfectly adequate for most sailplanes. It will operate rudder, elevator, ailerons and airbrakes. It has nicad rechargeable batteries. The four channel receiver with its aerial wire is alongside.

On the upper left is a much more expensive transmitter, with a built-in computer allowing individual adjustment for each control, several extra channels for auxiliaries such as flaps, undercarriage, aerotow release and special functions, and other elaborations. It also has memory to accept six different models, each with its own control set-up, and a screen to keep track of everything. The receiver is also shown.

The larger transmitter is more expensive again and has more facilities including over ninety model memories. Only the most dedicated enthusiast will ever need such a radio, and even this is not the most expensive!

worth considering is that if the radio is to be sold or traded in later, a four function set will be easier to dispose of because it will be of use to fliers of powered model aircraft as well as gliders – there will be more potential buyers for it.

BATTERIES

It is definitely worth spending extra in order to get a radio equipped with **nickel cadmium (nicad)** rechargeable batteries, and a **charger** for them. Ordinary dry batteries work when fresh but they must be replaced often. To have batteries running down while the model is flying is a sure way to lose it. In the long run this becomes more expensive than buying a nicad system in the first place. Dry batteries also give trouble sometimes by springing out of their retaining clips. If used they must at least be bound in place firmly with elastic bands or tape (the same applies to rechargeable nicad cells if these are bought separately. It is best to buy them already made up into packs with connectors ready to plug in).

Nicads can be charged overnight before a day's flying. Such batteries do not last for ever but with regular use and recharging they will serve for four to five years. They deteriorate more rapidly if not used. If the batteries have been standing idle for a year or two, do not expect them to be fit for use.

MORE FUNCTIONS?

Later gliders will have more than two controls. With **four function radio** the sailplane can have **ailerons** and **airbrakes** or **spoilers**. Although the cost will be more it is well worth worthwhile to pay the extra. Many glider pilots will never need more (the terms are explained later).

A likely price is £140. Once a good four function radio is bought it will last for years and can be used for many different models. A point

DON'T SPEND TOO MUCH!

Spending more than the minimum brings many advantages but it is probably best not to lay out too much on radio equipment until you know whether you are going to enjoy the sport. It is possible to spend a great deal on elaborate radio control gear. It does not follow that more money brings quicker success. The expert flier can buy an advanced system having ten or twelve functions, special switches and a built-in computer, with all kinds of extras such as 'model memories'. Such complex equipment is not easy to manage and is likely to increase the problems for a beginner.

If you become enthusiastic and want to move on to superior radios you will be able to recover some of the first costs by reselling. If, on the other hand, you decide after all to give up, you can still expect to sell. There is an active second-hand market.

The first radio should be bought as a complete set, which is cheaper than buying individual items separately. Some example prices for the various separate components are given below (The prices quoted are those prevailing at the time of writing. They vary from time to time according to economic conditions and international currency exchange rates.)

CHECK THE RADIO WITH A CLUB BEFORE BUYING

When buying the radio, especially if it is secondhand, consult the local model flying club to ensure that the **operating frequency** is legal and acceptable for use alongside other flying models. Some older secondhand, and some new but cheap radios, car and boat control equipment, or gear bought overseas, may not meet these criteria. Refer to the further remarks about radios in a later chapter.

CLUB SUBSCRIPTION

A very good initial investment is to pay a subscription to a model flying club. A good club will always have someone prepared to give instruction. There are, in most cases, reduced

rates for young people and costs are also reduced by sharing equipment. The club will have approved **flying sites** and will arrange **third party insurance** cover. Model gliders are not likely to injure anyone, but might do so. Damage to property, such as a car windscreen, is more possible therefore insurance is a wise precaution.

EXAMPLE RADIO EQUIPMENT COSTS (1997)

Complete set, 4 channel, £105 with dry batteries, £135 with nicads and charger.

TRANSMITTERS

4 channel transmitter only, no batteries, £40. With nicad batteries £56.

RECEIVERS

2 function, £24, 4 function, £30.

SERVOS

Standard servos £8 to £13 each (price varies with quality – gears metal or plastic, ball races, etc). Miniature servos for special uses cost more.

NICAD BATTERY PACKS

Prices vary with battery capacity. Typically about £10 for a 4.8 volt receiver pack, 600 mAh capacity. Transmitter battery packs, £17.

chapter three

COSTS:
THE FIRST GLIDER

Almost everyone begins by buying a basic kit for a suitable **two control training glider**, which should be less costly than the radio. There are many good kits priced at less than £50 and some as little as £22. If a kit costs more than £50 it should be of very high quality and be easy to put together. The kit will contain all the necessary wood and some pre-cut or preformed parts, with a plan and instructions to make assembly easy. The final result will be a robust aircraft which will take the radio gear easily and fly well. Complicated tools will not be needed and the model will go together in a relatively short time.

Do not be tempted to buy a very small model, in the mistaken belief that it will be easier to build and fly. As mentioned again later, a suitable model should have a **wing span** (the maximum distance from one wing tip to the other) between two and three metres, or around 7–9 ft. Much less than this makes the glider delicate, fiddly to construct and too easily upset in the air by gusts of wind or clumsy control movements.

ADDITIONAL COSTS

Most kits do not include glue or covering material for the wings, tail, etc., and a few additional items may be needed from the model shop. The final cost thus tends to creep up.

NO TIME TO SPARE?

Almost Ready To Fly (ARTF) models can be bought from the model shops. These are becoming very popular since although they are sometimes expensive they allow a beginner to get a model into the air in the shortest possible time. If time is reckoned as money, they are good value. A suitable model of the ARTF type is likely to cost about £75 and will require only two or three hours' work to fit the radio and get the glider ready for flight.

Whether to buy such a model depends chiefly on personal taste and interest. Traditionally, the sport of aeromodelling always included building as well as flying. There can be a lot of pleasure and interest in constructing the model and satisfaction in seeing it in the air.

Some people, however, find building models tiresome and want only to fly. There is nothing wrong with this. In sports such as golf and tennis no-one expects the player to make the equipment as well as using it. There is a place in model flying for everyone.

If ARTF models get broken it is not always easy to repair them because they may use various moulded plastic components which the amateur cannot deal with. The solution to such a problem may be to buy a spare part, such as a whole wing or fuselage.

Models may be bought completely **Ready to Fly (RTF)**. The cost will be quite high because the buyer is in effect paying someone else to build the model completely and even to fit the radio. The most important thing for the beginner who has the money to lay out is still to check with the local model flying club that the model will be suitable and will meet all the necessary criteria otherwise the cash will be wasted.

Offers of flying models and control gear for sale sometimes appear in the classified advertisements of daily or weekly papers. There are some bargains but before buying have everything examined and tested by an experienced person.

COMBINED DEALS

Model shops and mail order firms quite often put together combined deals, a model kit together with suitable radio, at a discounted price. It is obviously worth considering such offers.

Note: even when there are local manufacturers, some of the materials for a model may have to be imported from other countries. Since prices, international currency exchange rates and import duties change frequently, exact figures for these costs cannot be given. Expert advice from experienced people can be of assistance from the beginning. Failing this, an idea of prices can be gleaned by visiting a model shop or from the advertisements in the specialist model flying magazines, some of which are listed in Appendix 1.

TOOLS

A craft knife with some spare blades, some fine and medium grade abrasive papers, a small screwdriver, a small pair of pliers, a metal ruler and perhaps a few fine files and small gauge drill bits and a hand drill, a small, fine bladed saw, may have to be bought if not already available (Fig. 3.1). A razor plane and spare blades can be bought from a model shop. More expensive tools can be left until really needed later.

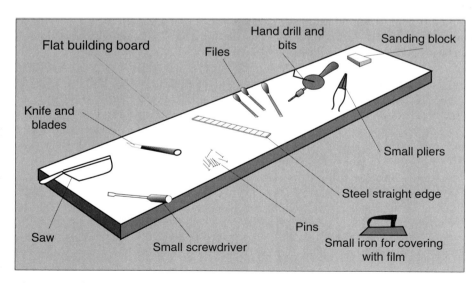

Figure 3.1 *Almost all the work required to build a simple two-control model glider can be done with the tools shown.*

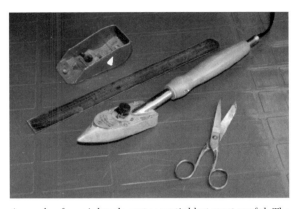

A couple of special tools, not essential but most useful. The razor plane in the background is used for shaping leading edges to smoothly rounded form. The electric iron with handle and adjustable temperature control is used for covering the model with the usual kind of plastic heat-shrinking film. Scissors and ruler give a scale for comparison.

BUILDING BOARD

For holding the wings, tail and fuselage straight while assembling and gluing, a flat board such as an old drawing board or a discarded table top, and some pins, will be used. The most important thing about the building board is that it should be flat and stay flat, without warps.

A piece of particle board of the kind sold for shelving, or heavy plywood, about 150cm long and 30cm wide, will do, but will be too hard for pins. One way to make it suitable is to cover it with 'pin-up' board material such as cork or something similar. The pins may be ordinary dressmakers' pins, but model shops sell special **T-shaped pins** which are more robust and easier to use. Pins with round glass or plastic heads are less useful, since the heads often break off, or the steel comes through the head when pushing a pin in! This can cause a painful spiking of a finger.

COVERING

For covering a model, **plastic film** is the most popular material. The film is stuck on and tightened by applying heat. Two rolls of the film should be enough for the first model with some left over. Get two bright and contrasting colours (see remarks about colours below). Save any spare film carefully for repairs and future models.

An old but serviceable electric **iron**, or a small travelling iron, will be required to stick the film onto the model framework. The sole of the iron may become stained, so do not use the best domestic iron for this, or at least clean it thoroughly afterwards. Special irons and **hot air guns** for covering are sold, but the first model can be built without them. It is possible to use a hair drier or even an electric radiator to shrink the covering, with care taken not to overheat the film which can be melted with too much heat. The iron used to stick the film on may be used for the shrinking, if this is done carefully.

Most of the gluing work on a beginner's model can be done with the commonplace white PVA **wood glue**. A very little two-part **epoxy resin glue** may be useful, and contact adhesive comes in handy occasionally. All these can be bought in ordinary hardware stores.

Cyanoacrylate or CA glue is very rapid setting and strong, so is now very popular. More is said about adhesives later.

SOMEWHERE TO WORK

Building a model requires space, preferably where dust and the odd spot of glue will do no harm. If there is no workshop available, a kitchen table can serve as a temporary workbench. The building board and tools can be cleared away at short notice. Protect floors or carpets with newspapers or plastic dust sheets.

Wear old clothes or a smock. Rub **barrier cream** on hands when using glues and paints.

POSSIBLE SAVINGS

Money, though not time, can be saved by building a model from scratch without a kit. Suitable **plans** are sold by the publishers of model flying magazines or alternatively friendly club members may lend drawings or give them away. The scratch builder then has to get the necessary materials together. Everything needed, sheets or strips of balsa, ply, pine or spruce, lengths of wooden dowelling or wire, will be obtainable from the same shop as the one selling kits and radios.

The disadvantage is that every separate part of the model will have to be made, which takes time and more skill than building from a kit. When the model is completed there may be some unused material lying around. This should never be wasted – it can be used on a future model, or for repairs and modifications.

chapter four

FIELD EQUIPMENT

THE FIELD KIT BOX

Keep some tools in a handy box so that they can be taken along with the model to the flying site. For emergency repairs, some quick setting glue (CA or so-called 5-minute epoxy) is a valuable field box item. Take some spare **rubber bands** if the model needs them, masking tape or insulating tape to make temporary repairs to punctured wing covering, scrap lead, and anything else that might be needed to overcome small problems on the field.

CLOTHING

No elaborate clothing is normally required when flying models. If the weather is very bad flying will be impossible in any case, and should not be attempted. Nonetheless, long periods will be spent out of doors, sometimes in exposed places, hilltops and coastal sites etc. A hat or cap to shade the eyes is a great help. Sunglasses should be worn and ultraviolet screen creams applied. In cold weather, wrap up well.

LAUNCHING APPARATUS

If the novice joins a club it should not be obligatory to buy any apparatus at first. For flights from a hilltop for slope soaring, the model will be launched by hand, and this is a good way to begin as no equipment is needed for this. For flying over flat land however, towline launching

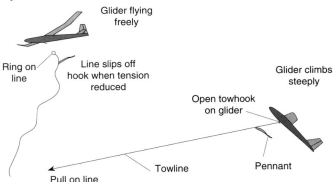

Figure 4.1 *The principles of launching a model sailplane are the same whether a hand tow, rubber bungee or winch is used.*

Glider flying freely

Ring on line

Line slips off hook when tension reduced

Glider climbs steeply

Open towhook on glider

Pull on line

Towline

Pennant

will normally be used and there is a need for some equipment. The club may or may not provide this.

For line launching, the glider has an open hook on the underside of its fuselage. A ring, such as an ordinary key ring, attaches the line temporarily to the glider, which is pulled up like a kite. The ring falls off the hook when the tension is slackened at the top of the launch. There is a pennant or a small parachute to help the pilot to see when the line has come off and to keep it straight as it falls (Fig. 4.1).

Ordinary light string or nylon cord may be used as a towline but monofilament fishing line is usually preferred. Fishermen's knots are essential for joining this type of line and repairing breaks (Figs 4.2 and 4.3).

THE HAND TOWLINE

Sometimes the best way of launching a glider is by hand towing (Fig. 4.4). The pilot needs the help of a runner to get his model up this way.

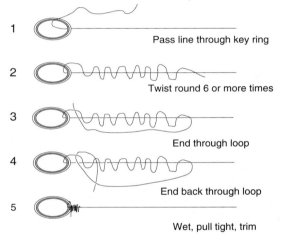

Figure 4.3 *Knot for attaching key ring to monofilament line.*

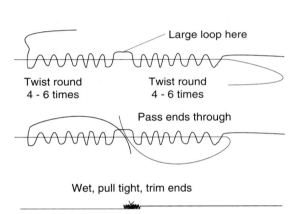

Figure 4.2 *Knot for joining broken monofilament line.*

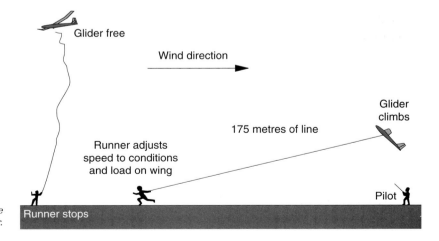

Figure 4.4 *Hand towline launch with runner.*

11

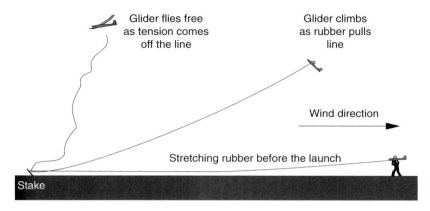

Glider flies free as tension comes off the line

Glider climbs as rubber pulls line

Wind direction

Stretching rubber before the launch

Stake

Figure 4.5 *The bungee or hi-start launch.*

Fishing line – 30kg (60lb) – is strong enough. The figures refer to the nominal breaking strain of the line. For competitions there is usually a limit on the length of line allowed to prevent anyone gaining an unfair advantage. A spool of some kind is needed to wind the line on when not in use. Wooden winding frames like those used for kite strings can be made easily. Special geared hand winches for towlines are available but are not cheap. These enable the line to be wound in very quickly after launching, which is required in competitions. A good hand towline launch can take the glider up to the full length of the line, ie 175 metres (574ft) from the ground.

THE BUNGEE OR HI-START LAUNCH

A method enabling the modeller to launch unaided is the so-called **bungee** or **hi-start** (Fig. 4.5). This is a 30 metre (100ft) length of rubber, preferably tubing or, second best, fabric-covered **rubber cord**, with 25–30kg (50–60lb) fishing line to make the total length to 150 metres (500ft), unstretched. A **stake** holds the far end of the rubber to the ground. A **hammer** will be needed in the field kit, to drive the stake in. The rubber is quite expensive and has to be replaced from time to time, as it perishes. To keep it longer store the bungee in a dark cupboard. A good club will have a bungee available always for members.

Complete bungees ready for use may be bought, and may cost between £30 and £40. It is cheaper to make one at home (Figs 4.6 and 4.7). This launching method is comparatively gentle and imposes less strain on the model and the pilot than any other method except the simple hand launch. More advice on launching is included in a later section of this book.

Towline

Keyring

Fishing swivel

Rubber tubing

Aluminium tube flattened and drilled

Tube glued and bound into end of rubber tube

Figure 4.6 *Components of a bungee or hi-start.*

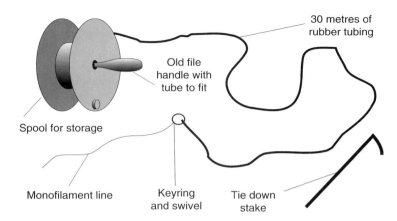

30 metres of rubber tubing

Old file handle with tube to fit

Spool for storage

Monofilament line

Keyring and swivel

Tie down stake

Figure 4.7 *The assembly of a bungee or hi-start.*

Launching apparatus. The spool carries a 30-metre length of rubber tubing and 120m fishing line with ring and pennant at the glider end. The stake and hammer are for fastening the end of the rubber to the ground.

This bungee will be used to launch Oscar Lansbury's two-control sailplane when the wings have been rubber-banded into place. Bungee or hi-start launching is very gentle and can be operated easily single-handed. On windless days it may not be entirely satisfactory.

WINCH LAUNCHING

A more sophisticated method of launching, suitable for all weathers, uses an electric-powered winch with a **turnaround pulley** and 400 metres (1312ft) total of line (Fig. 4.8). The winch is usually homemade using an old car starter motor and a 12V lead acid battery. Groups

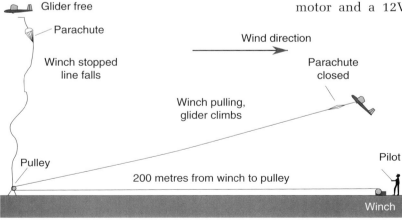

Glider free

Parachute

Winch stopped line falls

Wind direction

Parachute closed

Winch pulling, glider climbs

Pulley

Pilot

200 metres from winch to pulley

Winch

Figure 4.8 *Winch launching with a turnaround pulley.*

combine to design, build and pay for the winch, which can be quite expensive. For this reason it is common for clubs to own one or two winches for members to use.

The winch launch, unlike the bungee, can be quite fierce and unforgiving if the pilot makes a bad mistake or if the model is not strong enough to take the strain. Sometimes the winch can be adjusted to give gentler or faster launches according to need. The best way to learn is to get someone to help by operating the winch and launching the glider, while the pilot concentrates on controlling the model.

After a winch launch, the end of the line has to be pulled back for the next pilot to use it. This can be done by hand but many clubs, especially in the USA, use retrieving winches which bring the line back quickly with little effort.

Launching by winch, the winch motor and drum are in the box with a foot switch operated by the pilot (me). Lee Murray is about to launch the model. Winch launching can be much fiercer than the bungee and puts more strain on the model wings (photo: Jerry Slates).

AEROTOWING

Launching sailplanes by aerotowing, using a large powered model aeroplane as a tug, is becoming popular but is definitely not for beginners (Fig. 4.9). The towline is best attached to the tug near its balance point, and the glider has a special releasable coupling, normally in the extreme nose and worked by radio. The

A winch with a powerful starter motor and large accumulator, used for launching in competitions. Note the parachute to bring the line down without tangling, the foot switch in a wooden box and the hammer for staking the turnaround pulley firmly at the far end of the field (photo: David Morgan).

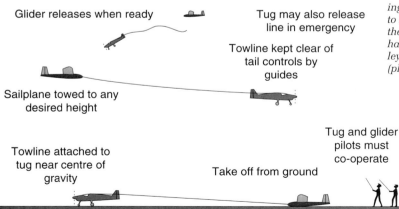

Glider releases when ready

Tug may also release line in emergency

Towline kept clear of tail controls by guides

Sailplane towed to any desired height

Towline attached to tug near centre of gravity

Take off from ground

Tug and glider pilots must co-operate

Figure 4.9 *Aerotowed launch requires a powerful tug aircraft and co-operative pilots.*

Aerotowed launching of large model sailplanes is quite common. It is not for beginners, but quite easy for the slightly more experienced pilot. This is a specialised tug aeroplane with a tow attachment just at the trailing edge of the wing and guide wires to keep the towline clear of the elevator and rudder controls. The tug motor is a 62cc four stroke which gives more power than strictly necessary.

powered model requires a safe pilot who understands the glider's needs, and the combination requires two radios working on two different frequencies to avoid mutual interference. Given these requirements, the sailplane can be launched with no danger to a height unobtainable by other launches.

chapter five

THE GLIDER: LAYOUT AND STRUCTURE

The diagrams illustrate the features of a simple model sailplane and name the parts (Fig. 5.1). A sketch of an advanced model is included to help the beginner recognise some of the things seen and talked about on the flying field (Fig. 5.2).

THE WING

The distance from tip to tip is the wing span or simply the span. A good span for a beginner's model is 2 to 2.5 metres (about 80 to 100 inches).

Smaller models than this are more difficult to build and tricky to control in rough air. The span has a very great influence on the behaviour and performance of the model. The span is also important when considering mundane things like getting the glider into the family car! To make wings easier to carry about, they often divide into two or more pieces. The two wings will be joined, possibly by steel rods sliding into brass or aluminium tubes.

The measurement directly across the wing from leading edge to trailing edge is called the

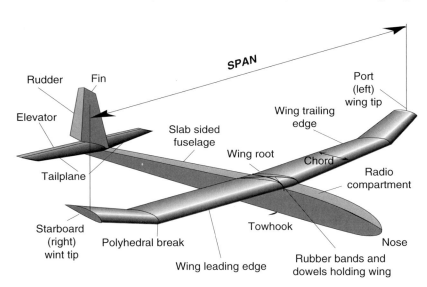

Figure 5.1 *A simple two-control training glider.*

16

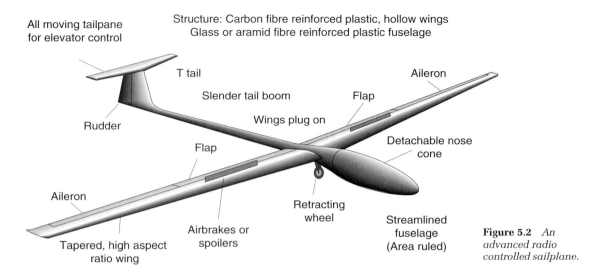

All moving tailpane for elevator control

Structure: Carbon fibre reinforced plastic, hollow wings
Glass or aramid fibre reinforced plastic fuselage

T tail

Aileron

Slender tail boom

Flap

Rudder

Wings plug on

Flap

Detachable nose cone

Aileron

Retracting wheel

Airbrakes or spoilers

Streamlined fuselage (Area ruled)

Tapered, high aspect ratio wing

Figure 5.2 *An advanced radio controlled sailplane.*

chord of the wing. This may be constant or the wing may be tapered.

The wing needs to be large and strong enough to support the whole weight of the glider without itself being very heavy. It is set on the fuselage at a small positive angle called the angle of incidence (Fig. 5.3). The tailplane is normally set at zero angle of incidence. Do not confuse these fixed angles with the angle of attack to the air, which is explained in a later chapter.

DIHEDRAL

If a glider is viewed from directly in front, it will be seen that in most cases the tips of the wings are higher than the root (Fig. 5.4). This upward angling is called dihedral. In some models the dihedral is continuous. The slope at the root continues unchanged to the tips. This is described as **straight dihedral**. In other cases the dihedral makes a fairly sharp change, increasing markedly toward the tips. This is called **polyhedral**. Aerobatic models often have no dihedral.

Very occasionally a model may be seen with curved dihedral. This makes construction difficult and does not seem to work any better than the simpler forms. The so-called gull wing was a common feature of full-sized sailplanes many years ago and may still be copied on models. There is a steep dihedral angle in the

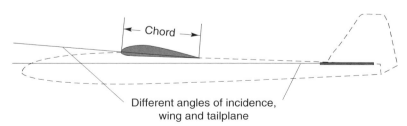

← Chord →

Different angles of incidence, wing and tailplane

Figure 5.3 *Angles of incidence. Note: the wing angle of incidence is measured from the true chord line which runs through the extreme leading and trailing edges. It is not correct to measure this angle from the bottom of the wing section.*

17

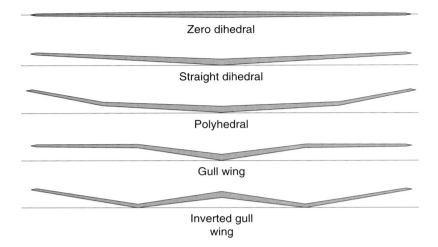

Zero dihedral

Straight dihedral

Polyhedral

Gull wing

Inverted gull
wing

Figure 5.4 *Types of dihedral.*

middle, then the outer parts of the wing curves to run horizontally or even slant slightly down (anhedral) toward the tips.

If control is by rudder and elevator only, like the typical beginner's model, much dihedral is required and polyhedral is common. If the dihedral is not enough, the rudder becomes ineffective, as explained in the section on the controls.

BUILT-UP WOODEN WINGS

Two main kinds of wing structure are in common use.

The traditional built-up framed structure is still preferred by many model fliers. There is a wooden **main spar**, running from the root to the tip and positioned about a third of the chord back from the leading edge (Fig. 5.5). This spar may be a simple strip of wood, or may be more

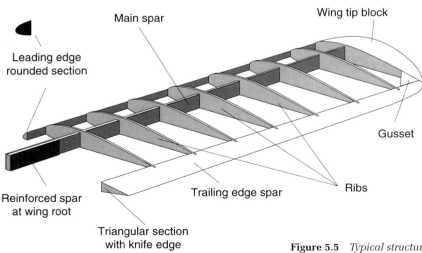

Main spar

Wing tip block

Leading edge
rounded section

Gusset

Reinforced spar
at wing root

Trailing edge spar

Ribs

Triangular section
with knife edge

Figure 5.5 *Typical structure of a built-up wooden wing.*

complicated, with top and bottom **flanges** and **webbing** between (Fig. 5.6). The main spar takes most of the bending loads. There may be a second spar further aft, which helps to cope with wing-twisting forces. Some wings have additional light multiple spars ahead of the main spar to give additional support to the covering. These may behave as **turbulators** (see glossary for an explanation).

Set crosswise will be a number of **wing ribs** shaped to give the wing its **aerofoil section** or **profile** (see below). In a kit, these ribs should be provided ready cut to shape with slots to fit the spars. A **trailing edge**, of triangular section, is glued to the ribs at their rear ends. The trailing edge should have a sharp rear edge rather than being blunt. The **leading edge**, which should be shaped round to make a smooth entry to the air, is glued to the front of the ribs. The wing tip may be formed by an extra thick rib, or by a block of balsa carved and sanded to a pleasing shape.

At the root end, spars will usually be doubled or strengthened in some way. Bending and twisting loads at the centre of the wing are large, so it is always important to build the wings strongly in the centre. Such a wing will probably be covered with plastic film, stuck on by the pressure of a moderately hot iron and shrunk by heat to give a smooth, airtight skin. Some of the wing may be skinned with sheet balsa wood. The plastic film goes over this too.

A built-up wing is almost always repairable after damage. Spars and leading or trailing edges can be re-joined and strengthened if they crack. New ribs can be cut out from sheet balsa of the same thickness and weight as the original. The covering can be patched. After repairs the wing should be as strong as ever, although often a little heavier. The extra weight is not necessarily serious although some re-balancing may be required.

FOAM-CORED WINGS

The second very popular type of wing has a core of **expanded polystyrene** or some other foamed plastic material (Fig. 5.7). Onto this a **veneer** of balsa, obechi, very thin (0.4 mm) plywood, or a layer of glass cloth is glued, with leading edges and tips added and internal reinforcements in places of high stress such as the roots.

In most kits the foam-cored wing is provided with skins already glued on. In other cases the core is provided bare, packed between the remnants of the block it was originally cut from (the **sleeve**), with sufficient sheet wood to finish. The sleeve pieces should be kept, since they are necessary to complete the skinning process and for repairs. The adhesive chosen to glue veneers to the plastic requires care because some glues will dissolve the foam. The instructions with the kit should cover these points. If not, seek advice before starting.

After the skin is on, it is still important not to allow paints, thinners or any other liquids or

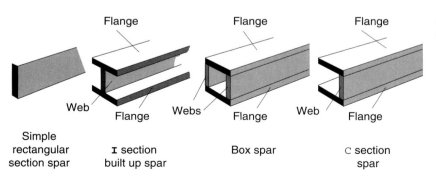

Flange   Flange   Flange

Web   Flange   Webs   Flange   Web   Flange

Simple rectangular section spar   I section built up spar   Box spar   C section spar

Figure 5.6 *Types of wooden main spar.*

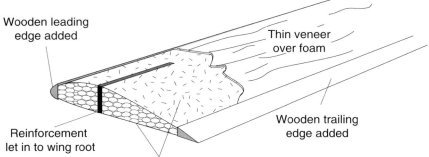

Wooden leading edge added

Thin veneer over foam

Reinforcement let in to wing root

Wooden trailing edge added

Foamed plastic core cut to section with hot wire between templates or computer controlled

Figure 5.7 *A foam plastic-cored, wooden-skinned wing.*

vapours of the wrong kind, to penetrate to the underlying plastic, which they can do even through a thin sheet of wood.

A veneered wing can be covered with heat-shrinking plastic film, but other treatments are possible, including skinning with light glass cloth and epoxy resin, smoothing and painting. **Polyester resins**, on the other hand, attack the plastic foam and **should not be used**.

Such wings are very robust and will stand more abuse than the built-up variety. They may survive unharmed in crashes which would break a built-up wing but they tend to be slightly heavier.

Foam-cored wings can be repaired unless they have suffered extensive crushing. Small dents can be filled in and sanded, to be repainted or re-covered. Larger dents can be cut out, new pieces of foam glued in and shaped, and the skin or edge member replaced. If,

however, the wing breaks right across near the root, with little chance of restoring the original strength, it is often best to make a completely new wing. This may entail buying new foam cores, since cutting the plastic accurately with a hot wire requires a certain amount of expertise and some equipment. Someone in the club will know how it is done!

THE TAIL UNIT

The tail is really a small set of wings whose work may be likened to that of the fletching on an arrow, keeping the glider heading into the airflow and also directing the flight (Fig. 5.8).

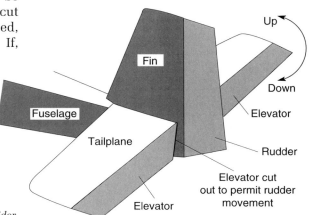

Up

Fin

Down

Fuselage

Elevator

Tailplane

Rudder

Elevator cut out to permit rudder movement

Elevator

Figure 5.8 *The tail unit of a simple glider.*

The horizontal **tailplane**, often called the **stabiliser** (stab for short), is there to balance and damp down or stabilise any up and down pitching. In straight and level flight the tailplane operates at a slightly negative angle relative to the wing. The **elevator** controls nose up and nose down motion and hence the flight speed and glide angle. Some models have a fixed tailplane to which the elevator is hinged. In other cases, an all moving or **slab tailplane** (in some older texts called a **pendulum elevator**) is able to pivot about a crosswise rod, so the entire tailplane surface becomes also the elevator.

The vertical tail surface or **fin** stabilises side-to-side yawing motions. The **rudder** is hinged to the fin and is used to yaw the glider to left or right as required by the pilot.

The tail is lightly built but it has to be strong enough to do its job even at high speeds when the controls are being operated, and to survive the occasional heavy landing.

THE FUSELAGE

The **fuselage** exists mainly to house and protect the radio gear and to join the wing and tail of the glider together (Fig. 5.9).

Fuselages take a lot of punishment even when the model is well flown. Model gliders do not often have any real undercarriage but land on the belly. Even in a perfect landing the model slides along the ground and may scrape against stones and gravel or even concrete. In bad landings it is the fuselage which hits hardest. It also provides the attachment point for the towhook which comes under strain during launching. Fuselages have to be strong and are quite heavily built by comparison with the wing. The front part where the radio gear is, and often some heavy trimming ballast too, tends to burst open. Another common point of breakage is at the rear, just in front of the tail.

A beginner's kit will normally provide materials for a squarish or **slab-sided** wooden fuselage. This will be a long, narrow box, with sides, top and bottom of sheet balsa wood, probably strengthened at vital points with plywood doublers and **cross frames** or **formers**, and **longerons** running from nose to tail. There will be compartments ahead of the wing for the trim ballast, battery, receiver and servos, and control **pushrods** will run through to the tail. Details of how to fit all this in will depend slightly on the type of radio and control rods to be used. Advice appears in a later chapter.

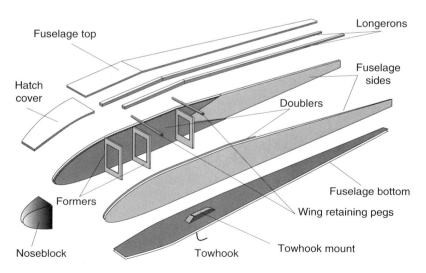

Fuselage top

Longerons

Hatch cover

Fuselage sides

Doublers

Formers

Fuselage bottom

Wing retaining pegs

Noseblock

Towhook

Towhook mount

Figure 5.9 *The components of a typical wooden, slab-sided fuselage.*

The instructions with the kit may recommend skinning the front of the fuselage with **glass cloth**, mainly to resist wear in landing and the occasional heavy blows. It is worth doing this, if possible, even if the instructions do not mention it.

If the wings are to be held on with rubber bands, which is a very popular and reliable method, wooden dowels will be fitted just behind and just in front of the wing to make a secure anchorage. It is wise always to use about six bands on such a wing, in case some of them snap in the air.

Otherwise the fuselage may provide for wings to plug on. In these cases some way of preventing them working loose in flight is required. There may be a pair of hooks on the wing root ribs, allowing a stretched rubber band to pass through inside the fuselage and pull the wings together, or a spring clip of some type may be used. Some modellers rely simply on electrical tape to hold the wings together but this marks the model and may strip the wing covering. A detachable hatch cover or canopy will be required, to allow access to the radio and the switch if this is internally mounted.

Mounting the switch externally is easy and makes for convenience, but it has been known for a pilot or helper to knock the switch off accidentally just before launching. It is slightly safer to have the switch inside the receiver or battery compartment so that access to it is obtained only by removing the hatch cover. In either case, make quite sure the switch is on before every flight!

chapter six

SOME FINER POINTS OF DESIGN

Apart from the rudder and elevator, more advanced sailplanes have **ailerons** on the wings and **airbrakes** and **flaps** as well. A beginner's model will usually not have these – their use will be learned later. Model gliders with ailerons do not need much dihedral and aerobatic models may have none at all.

Wings may sometimes be swept back or swept forward. This is often done merely for the sake of fashion and style. There is little other advantage in either form of sweep. Sweep does affect the required position of the balance point of the model.

WING AREA AND ASPECT RATIO

The **total area** of a wing (or tail surface) always includes any part of the fuselage or body of the

glider which lies between the two halves of the wing. A wing with a large area and small span appears very broad. This is a **low aspect ratio** wing. A narrow wing with large span, has a **high aspect ratio** (Fig. 6.1). Up to a point, high aspect ratio (long, narrow) wings create less drag than those with low aspect ratio, but they are also more flexible, can twist or even vibrate rapidly (flutter) in flight, and are more easily damaged. For these reasons beginners' models have only moderate aspect ratio wings.

TAPERED WINGS

Wings may be tapered in plan so that the chord at the tip or outer end is less than the inner end or root (Fig. 6.2). This has structural advantages since it reduces the bending stresses and also

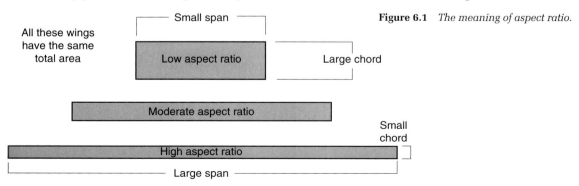

Figure 6.1 *The meaning of aspect ratio.*

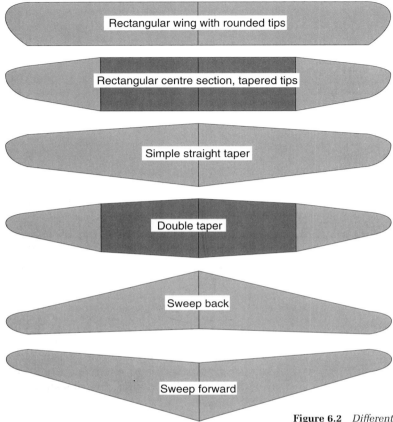

Rectangular wing with rounded tips

Rectangular centre section, tapered tips

Simple straight taper

Double taper

Sweep back

Sweep forward

Figure 6.2 *Different forms of wing taper and sweep.*

gives more depth of wing at the root end for strong spars. There is some saving in drag too. Tapered wings are harder to build than plain rectangular ones, so many beginners' models avoid them. Tapering the outer panels of the wing, leaving the inner section rectangular, is a good compromise. Other types of taper are illustrated in the diagram. The theoretical ideal, hardly ever seen, is an elliptical plan. It is not advisable to make the wing tips too narrow, so they are usually finished off fairly square.

WARPS AND WASHOUT

Both wings must be the same if the glider is to fly straight. Check carefully before flying to see that there is no unintended twist which will cause one wing to lift more than the other. Ways of correcting this fault, or better still, preventing it, are mentioned in the section on building the model.

A wing may be built with some deliberate twist, called **washout** (Fig. 6.3) This is introduced by blocking the trailing edge up towards the tips during construction. The angle of incidence of the outer wing is slightly reduced, taking some of the lift load in flight away from

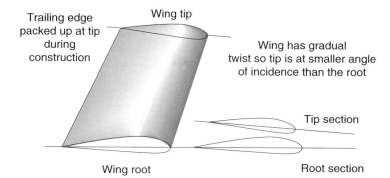

Trailing edge packed up at tip during construction

Wing tip

Wing has gradual twist so tip is at smaller angle of incidence than the root

Tip section

Wing root

Root section

Figure 6.3 *The meaning of washout.*

the tips and transferring it inwards along the wing. There is less chance then of **tip stalling** during flight, which causes the model to tilt over as one wing loses lift and drops sharply (**stalling** occurs if the airflow over the wing breaks away,

reducing the lift). Whether or not the plans call for washout, its opposite, wash-in, with the twist the other way, is to be avoided.

There is a difference between building a wing deliberately with washout, and introducing a warp by accident. Advice on this appears later.

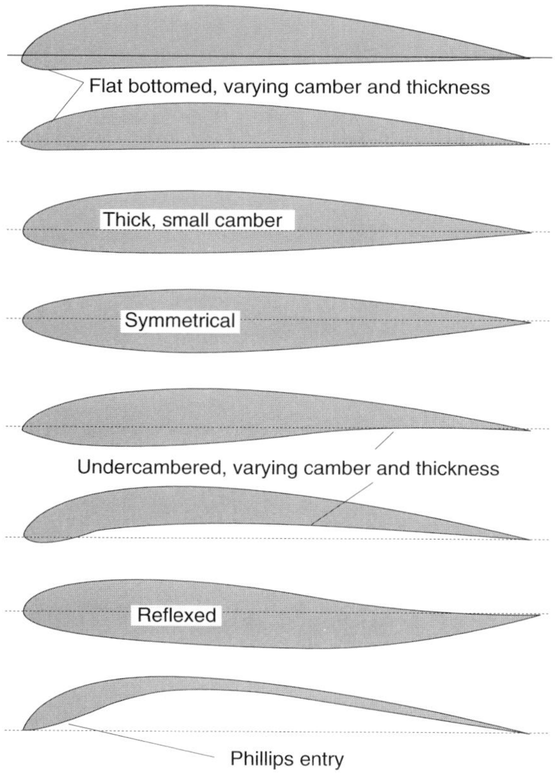

Flat bottomed, varying camber and thickness

Thick, small camber

Symmetrical

Undercambered, varying camber and thickness

Reflexed

Phillips entry

Figure 6.4 *Some types of wing section.*

WING SECTIONS

The **wing section**, **wing profile**, **aerofoil** or **airfoil section** of a wing is the shape seen if the wing is cut through chordwise (Fig. 6.4). If the wing is of the built-up kind, the ribs show this shape. The section on a beginner's model will usually be the same all the way along the wing, but more advanced designs often change in profile from root to tip. The tail surfaces also have aerofoil sections, usually very thin and symmetrical. Among model glider fliers there is probably more argument about wing sections than any other aspect of model design.

WING SECTION THICKNESS

To summarise the main points, a thin wing section is likely to perform better than a thick one but will require accurate control in flight to get the most out of it. It is not easy to make a thin wing strong, stiff and light. Thick wing sections are more forgiving but lack the competitive edge.

Thicknesses of wing sections are expressed as percentages. The maximum thickness is measured and divided by the chord distance. The result is multiplied by 100. A wing 7% thick is thin by model glider standards – 15% would count as thick. Tail sections are always very thin.

CAMBER

The next most important feature of a wing section is its **camber**, which is its general curvature or arching (Fig. 6.5). A line midway between the upper surface and lower surface of the wing section is drawn and this curve is compared with the straight chord line drawn directly from the extreme leading edge to the trailing edge, as shown in the diagram.

The camber line may be thought of as the **skeleton** of the aerofoil section, and it determines many of the most important features of the wing's flight behaviour. The rest of the wing can be thought of as the flesh added round the skeleton. The maximum distance of the central line from the chord line, is the camber, which is measured, like the thickness, as a percentage of the chord.

Most model glider wings have some upward or positive camber, between 1% and 6%, the latter figure being unusually high. A high camber makes for good performance at low speeds and a slow landing, but such a wing creates a lot of unwanted air resistance or drag in fast flight. A typical beginner's model will probably have about 3% camber, which is a compromise between the requirements of fast and slow flight.

WING SECTION NAMES

In conversation the beginner will often hear terms like flat-bottomed, semi-symmetrical, undercambered and perhaps Phillips entry, all relating to wing sections.

A **flat-bottomed section** is one with most of the underside flat. Beginners' models nearly always have flat-bottomed wing sections because they are easy to build, but this does not mean they have no camber. The camber is always measured from the true chord line to the curved mid-section line. A thick wing with a flat bottom has more centreline camber than a thin flat bottomed one, so the mere fact of both being flat underneath is not very significant. It is the form of the centreline skeleton that counts in the air.

An **undercambered** wing has the underside arched upwards, giving a concave form. This

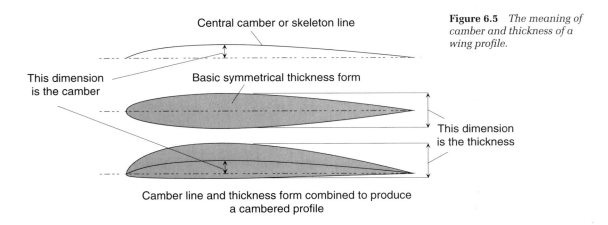

Central camber or skeleton line

This dimension is the camber

Basic symmetrical thickness form

This dimension is the thickness

Camber line and thickness form combined to produce a cambered profile

Figure 6.5 *The meaning of camber and thickness of a wing profile.*

makes construction and covering the wing more difficult. The covering material has to be thoroughly stuck to the underside of the wing structure or it will pull away as it tightens. The camber is measured in the same way as before, using the central skeleton line.

A glider intended specially for aerobatics might have no camber. The chord line and the skeleton line are then the same, perfectly straight. Such a wing section is **symmetrical** with exactly the same curvature on both upper and lower surfaces. This enables it to fly upside down or right way up with equal ease, but the performance in other respects is not so good. Tail units usually have symmetrical sections, though not always.

So-called semi-symmetrical wing sections have the lower surface somewhat less outwardly curved than the upper side. The true camber is still measured the same way, from the central curved line to the straight chord line.

Semi-symmetrical is a confusing term which really ought not to be used. A wing is either cambered by some amount like 1% or 3%, or it is fully symmetrical. Whether it is convex underneath, flat or undercambered depends on how the central skeleton line curve happens to combine with the thickness. A thickish wing with a fairly large camber, may still appear convex on both sides, whereas a thin wing with the same camber may come out undercambered.

Horatio Phillips was a pioneer of aviation who did some famous experiments with wing sections before 1890. His work was valid in its time but has been long superseded. Anyone describing a wing as having a Phillips entry is more than 100 years behind the times! It is not tactful for a beginner to mention this to senior club members!

SECTION NAMES AND NUMBERS

Beyond the terms mentioned above, aerofoil sections (airfoil sections in the USA) have names or numbers, such as **Clark Y, Göttingen 795, NACA 4412, HQ 1.5/9, Girsberger RG 15, Selig 3021, SD 7037** and so on almost without end. The names indicate the designer or research organisation that developed the particular section. For instance, Clark was a US Navy scientist who developed a range of sections in the early 1920s. The letters NACA stand for the National Advisory Council for Aeronautics, also of the USA; Göttingen sections came from Göttingen University; Rolf Girsberger, Michael Selig and Helmut Quabeck are model fliers and designers.

Glider fliers are constantly trying new sections and there is a lot of accumulated experience. Wind tunnel tests and computer runs have been done on profiles in search of better ones. This experimentation is part of the interest of model gliding.

STREAMLINED FUSELAGES

The performance of a sailplane depends greatly on the **drag** or resistance of the air as it flies. The more the drag, the worse the glide. To save a little drag, the fuselage may be streamlined. Such fuselages can be made from wood. One simple way of doing this is to round off the corners of a slab-sided shape. Some kits include a very refined plastic moulded fuselage of **glass cloth reinforced plastic** (GRP) or other plastic. Supports are glued in place for the radio, wing and tail. It is not even essential to paint such a unit, which may already be finished in white or coloured. Such fuselages are also sold separately, to be fitted with wings of any kind preferred. They can be repaired after damage, as a rule, but special materials and adhesives may be required.

TAIL UNITS

The first model will probably have the fin and rudder mounted above the tailplane. If the elevator is of the all-moving type it will probably be mounted partway up the fin. The **T-tail** arrangement is also quite common. The tailplane is mounted at the extreme top of the fin, making a letter T. One advantage is that the tailplane is taken out of the wake of the fuselage and wing, so becomes more efficient. The structure of the fin and rear fuselage requires strengthening, which adds some weight.

Although not recommended for a beginner's model, the **V-tail** layout is quite popular. In this, there are two surfaces arranged in a V fashion instead of vertical fin and horizontal tailplane. Some weight and drag may be saved this way. To get both elevator and rudder action, the controls have to be coupled so that, for pitch control, both surfaces go up and down together, and for yawing, both move the same way, left or right. The required linkage may be done mechanically in the glider, or in the transmitter, electronically.

chapter seven

THE RADIO CONTROL GEAR

The model flier can operate modern radio control gear without any knowledge of radio or electronics, except for a few very important things like ensuring that the equipment is switched on, batteries fully charged, wires not about to break, and miniature plugs properly inserted. Flat batteries and broken wires are probably the chief cause of loss of control of model gliders. Launching the model without switching the radio on is also more common than it should be.

Assuming all such details have been attended to, the pilot operates the **transmitter** (commonly abbreviated to **Tx**) which translates movements of thumbs and fingers into coded signals, actually a series of high speed digital impulses or 'bleeps', imposing these on, or modulating, the radio signal from the aerial.

The **receiver** (**Rx**), in the model, tuned to the appropriate frequency, picks up the signals coming in through its own **aerial**, decodes them and passes them to the small electric **servo motors** which, in turn, respond with a mechanical movement (Fig. 7.1). The servo arms are connected, by pushrods or cables, to the controls of the glider.

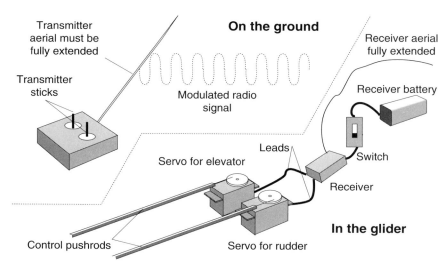

Transmitter aerial must be fully extended

On the ground

Receiver aerial fully extended

Transmitter sticks

Modulated radio signal

Receiver battery

Leads

Switch

Servo for elevator

Receiver

Control pushrods

Servo for rudder

In the glider

Figure 7.1 *The components of a two function radio control outfit.*

Modern radios are **crystal controlled**. A small wafer of crystal is ground very accurately to thickness and housed in a case. One is plugged into the oscillating circuit of the transmitter and a matching one in the receiver. The crystals vibrate at a set rate and fix the frequency very exactly.

The crystals look like small two-pinned plugs and fit into sockets so that they can be changed when necessary (Fig. 7.2). A receiver with the wrong crystal for its transmitter, or no crystal at all, will not work. It is best to leave the crystals in their sockets as much as possible since damage can be done by too much handling. They can, however, be changed quite quickly to alter the operating frequency of the radio. This is useful if many people are trying to operate on the same channel at a particular site. In some competitions it is required for everyone to have an alternative set of crystals.

TWO FUNCTION TRANSMITTERS

For a two channel or two function set of radio control equipment there will be a self-contained transmitter, small and light enough to be held in the hands (Fig. 7.3). It will have an on/off switch and an access panel to allow for changing the batteries. The crystal may be accessible from outside but more likely will be hidden inside the case. If nicad batteries are fitted there will be a socket for the charger. A small meter or at least a light will indicate whether the set is switched on. The telescopic aerial requires to be screwed or clipped on and must be fully extended when the set is in use.

In some older transmitters, switching on without the aerial could cause damage, but modern equipment avoids this.

On the face of the transmitter will be two control levers or **sticks**, one capable of moving back and forth, the other side to side. The right-hand stick will be the one which moves sideways and this is for working the rudder on the glider, **stick to the right for right rudder** and **stick left for left rudder**. When the glider is **viewed from behind**, right rudder means the rudder goes to the right as the transmitter stick also goes to the right. Stick left, rudder left. When connecting the controls of the glider, make sure this is correct. The left-hand stick then is for the **elevator**. The **elevator goes down when the stick moves forward**; stick back, elevator up. Springs return both sticks quickly to the central position if they are released. Close to each stick will be a small slide switch for trimming.

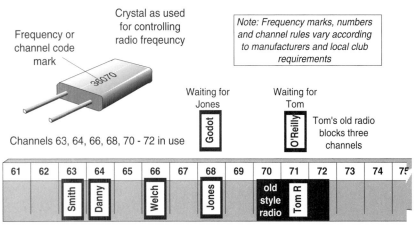

Note: Frequency marks, numbers and channel rules vary according to manufacturers and local club requirements

Figure 7.2 *A frequency control board as used by some model flying clubs.*

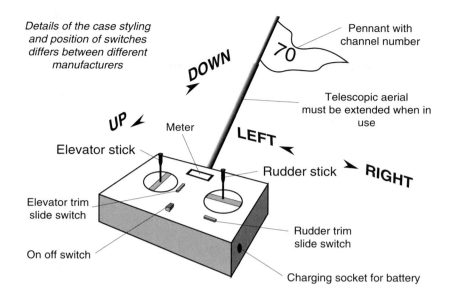

Details of the case styling and position of switches differs between different manufacturers

DOWN

UP

Meter

LEFT

Elevator stick

Pennant with channel number

Telescopic aerial must be extended when in use

Rudder stick

RIGHT

Elevator trim slide switch

On off switch

Rudder trim slide switch

Charging socket for battery

Figure 7.3 *The transmitter.*

FOUR FUNCTION TRANSMITTERS

On a four channel set the two sticks will be mounted on universal gimbals for movement in any direction. The centring springs are fitted as before, except that the fore–aft motion of one stick will be governed by a ratchet. In the forward and back direction, this stick will remain in any position without automatic re-centring. With gliders, this stick may be used to control airbrakes or spoilers (in powered models it works the engine throttle). Radios with more than four functions retain the same kind of sticks. The extra functions are then controlled by switches and special buttons.

RADIO FREQUENCIES

Clubs are usually careful to check any radio transmitter that will be operated at the flying field, to certify that it is within legal limits. The wavebands permitted for radio control equipment vary from country to country but most radios can be retuned to suit the local situation but new crystals will be needed. (27 Mhz is not often used for models now because of interference from Citizen's Band radios. This should be remembered if very old radio gear appears on the secondhand market.)

KNOW YOUR CHANNEL NUMBER

Within the broad wavebands allocated to model flying, many separate channels can be fitted, allowing a number of models to be flown at the same time. The precise frequency of each model is determined by the crystal and on any flying day at a particular site, it is probable that several pilots will have radios on the same channel. If two transmitters are switched on simultaneously on identical channels, they interfere with one another, causing one or both models to crash. A club should have a system for preventing this but cannot predict the occasional thoughtless action (see Fig. 7.2). Avoiding mutual interference depends on controlling all transmitters at a particular flying site. Anyone who switches on a transmitter without first

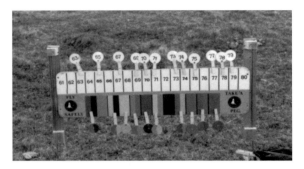

A clothes' peg system used to avoid frequency clashes at a popular model flying site. Ivinghoe Beacon in Bedfordshire. The pilot takes a peg with the channel number and clips it to the transmitter aerial. No-one else is then permitted to switch on a transmitter on that channel.

clear, that spot must be reserved by placing a named and numbered tag or key on the board. No-one should switch a transmitter on unless their key is in place. Remove the tag quickly when the channel is no longer required and the transmitter off, to let someone else use it. Another popular method is to have a sort of totem pole or stave marked with all the channel numbers with a series of clothes' pegs clipped one above the other, each carrying a disc with the channel number. The flier wishing to operate a transmitter takes the appropriate peg and clips it to the transmitter aerial. Nobody operates a Tx if the peg is not in place.

In large meetings or contests, a system of keeping all transmitters in a **pound** is used, the only ones allowed out are those to be used immediately for a flight.

ensuring that the frequency is clear, is likely to become very unpopular in a very short time, and may even be held financially responsible for damaging someone else's model. Do not, for example, switch the transmitter on 'just for a quick check', even with the aerial down, in the car park before taking the model out to fly.

Make sure the exact frequency of the transmitter crystal is known and, if it is not already marked, write it down clearly and label the transmitter case. If there is some doubt, a typical crystal should have its frequency marked in small figures on the side of its case, such as 27.785 in the 27 Mhz range, or 35.050 in the 35 Mhz band. The club, or the model shop, should have a list of the associated channel numbers. Radios usually come with a small pennant with the correct number, to be attached to the transmitter aerial. There is much to be said for making such a pennant if it is not provided.

If, for any reason, the crystals are changed to another channel, make sure this is noted and correctly labelled and the pennant changed.

Various systems of frequency control are in use. The club may set up a board with all the available channels marked and numbered. Anyone wishing to switch on a transmitter checks the board first. If the required channel is

THE RECEIVER

The receiver in its case with an **aerial** wire (which must be **uncoiled** to lie or be suspended straight in flight) will have sockets for the servos, battery and crystal to plug into. The instruction book will explain which socket is for which and these may also be marked or numbered on the receiver.

There will be a simple on/off slide switch, with wiring harness and plugs to connect the receiver to the battery. The plugs and sockets normally are 'keyed' to prevent wrong connections.

SERVOS

In a first set of equipment the servos will be of standard size. Later, smaller, lighter and more expensive ones may be obtained, or servos with ball bearings which respond more quickly and precisely, or larger servos with more power for bigger models.

OPERATING RANGE

Given fully charged batteries and with all the equipment in good condition, a model glider can be controlled in the air until it becomes difficult to see. The model will be out of sight before the radio range is exceeded. It is of course very risky to let a model get so far away. It is very easy to lose control simply by being unable to see what the model is doing.

However, various things can cause a model to go out of range while still in sight. If the aerials are not extended this cuts the range down to a very short distance. Make sure the aerials on both the transmitter and the receiver are fully extended before flying.

With long use, the transmitter aerial may become loose in its socket, or the joints can develop electrical faults, either of which can cause loss of range. Have the aerial checked from time to time.

If the receiver aerial is run loosely inside the fuselage of the glider a heavy landing can cause it to bunch up to the front and if this is not discovered the next flight becomes a disaster. The fine aerial wire can get broken too. Inspect it to make sure this has not happened.

Some kinds of paint, especially with lead or other metallic content, on the fuselage can shield the receiver aerial. Some materials, such as carbon fibre, also prove to have bad effects and some model fliers have had trouble with metal control pushrods and cables. For all these reasons, the receiver aerial is best arranged to lie outside the fuselage, either taped to the side or stretched lightly to the top of the fin.

GROUND TESTING

It is wise, before flying, to do a ground check of range. This should be explained in the instruction book sold with the radio gear, and is done by getting someone to hold the model off the ground while the pilot walks away from it with the transmitter, operating the sticks to see if the controls are, or are not, working correctly. Any defect in the system usually shows up as a rapid 'chattering' with the servos running to one extreme position and staying there. If the cause of this cannot be found and corrected easily, do not risk flying but have everything checked by a qualified radio servicer.

INTERFERENCE

Interference between radios is still possible in some circumstances, even between different channels. A cheap transmitter, for instance, may tend to swamp the adjacent channels on either side. In this case, the club will require the member to use a wide key on the frequency control board, or three pegs if the peg system is used, so that all the channels affected are closed while this radio is operating. One of the points to ask about when buying a radio, is whether it will be acceptable in this respect.

Interference can also arise, though rarely, due to harmonic effects between two transmitters even though they are widely separated on the frequency board. It is **risky** at any time to fly a model very **close to someone else's operating transmitter**, since occasional breaking through of the signal can occur.

INTERFERENCE FROM OTHER SOURCES

If someone is working a radio controlled **model car** or a **boat** and a glider on the same channel flies nearby, the glider will crash. This is particularly worrying since the sailplane may easily fly several hundred metres away from its transmitter and can pick up signals from a source quite unsuspected by the pilot. Cars and boats do sometimes operate on the same channels as aircraft.

Occasionally model pilots have complained of harmonic interference from such things as paging systems in nearby offices or hospitals. Modern radios rarely suffer from this.

CONTROL MODES

Some glider pilots fly with the elevator control worked by the left hand and directional control by the right. This is called **Mode 1** (Fig. 7.4). Two function radio gear is usually set up this way, and those who have learned on such equipment may prefer to stay with Mode 1 afterwards. Airbrakes might be operated by the right-hand stick.

Most pilots who begin with four function radios adopt **Mode 2**. The elevator and directional control are both worked by the right-hand stick.

Although there is much argument, there really is not much reason to prefer one mode to the other. Mode 1 is liked by many simply because it separates the two main functions. Mode 2 appeals to people who have experience in full-sized flying since the single control column of any full-sized light aircraft or sailplane works both elevator and ailerons, with throttle or brakes on the left side of the cockpit.

Transmitters can be adjusted for either mode. It is usually easy to change the ratchet and centr-

ing springs round to suit the pilot. Which mode is used will probably depend on the preferences of the instructor who teaches the beginner to fly. It is possible to change over later.

TYPES OF RADIO

Most four channel radio transmitters will have switches, preferably inside the case, which allow the servos' direction of action to be reversed. This is useful if a particular model has the servos awkwardly placed for operation or if the controls cannot be connected easily. It is very important, of course, that the switches are set correctly for the model concerned. If the radio gear is moved from one model to another, make absolutely sure that movement switches are correct.

Other adjustments which may be possible on more costly transmitters, such as exponential control action, trim centring, control limits and coupling, are not necessary at first and can be left alone for the first model at least.

Some of the technical terms applied to radios may puzzle the beginner. Providing the radio set is bought complete from a reputable model shop there will be no serious problems arising from this. Advice will be given if asked for.

If the various units are bought separately,

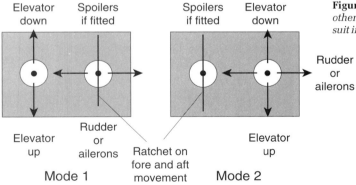

Figure 7.4 *Transmitter control modes. Note that other modes are possible, and may be arranged to suit individual preferences, e.g. for left-handed pilots*

however, it is necessary to make sure that a particular receiver is compatible with a particular transmitter.

Some manufacturers go to a lot of trouble to make their units interchangeable with other products. A receiver of one make will often work perfectly with a transmitter from another manufacturer. In other cases the match will not be quite so good and at least one of the major manufacturers has a system entirely different from the rest.

The mismatching extends even to the small connecting plugs which join the various components in the model. Fortunately the connectors themselves can usually be swapped, with a little soldering work, and servos, batteries and switches are then almost wholly interchangeable. This is not so with the main items, transmitters and receivers.

As with ordinary domestic radios, the model control apparatus may be either AM or FM. The letters stand for **amplitude modulation** and **frequency modulation**. Amplitude modulation was at one time the only type of radio available and units of this type are still quite popular and slightly cheaper than the others. FM came later and has some advantages. From the model flier's viewpoint the most important is relative freedom from interference.

Other letters that may be attached to more expensive radios are PCM and PPM, **pulse code modulation** and **pulse position modulation**. The technical meaning and the advantages of each are not specially important for the beginner but it is necessary to make sure the transmitter and receiver are both the same, ie both PCM or both PPM. A PPM receiver will not work with a PCM transmitter, and vice versa. The more expensive transmitters can be switched from one system to the other but ordinary four function transmitters cannot. Check all these points before buying.

chapter eight

BUILDING THE MODEL

It is not possible here to give detailed advice about building a particular model but some general points and hints which may not appear on the plan or in the instructions in the kit, will be mentioned.

PLANS AND INSTRUCTIONS

One of the things to consider when buying a kit is whether the **plans** and **instructions** included seem good enough. Often they are not satisfactory but this does not necessarily mean the model itself will be poor. Some otherwise good kits are sold with very little in the way of drawings and explanatory instructions. If no help is available, it is worth spending a little more money to get a kit which is well documented. What may be needed otherwise is more help from an experienced model builder.

CHECK THE KIT

Go through the kit carefully. Examine the material supplied, making sure it is adequate. If not, go back to the supplier, point out the faults, and get a replacement.

The kind of thing to look for is any **badly sawn** piece of balsa or other wood, such that it has been split or cut seriously under or over size (Fig. 8.1). Sometimes the saw marks on a thin piece of wood are so deep that it will crack when under strain. Occasionally a piece of sheet balsa will have one edge much thicker than the other, so the whole sheet is useless.

The **grain** of strip wood intended for spars or longerons should be generally **straight** and run along the full length of the strip. If it veers off at a sharp angle across the strip, which is called short grain, or shows knots and twists, the strength of that member will be reduced. Absolute perfection with a natural material like wood is not possible. A small defect may be acceptable if it can be placed in an unimportant part of the structure.

Some slight **winding** or **warping** of the longer pieces of wood is almost inevitable and need not be cause for alarm unless it is obviously very bad, in which case the shop should replace it.

Balsa wood is highly **variable**. One piece can be three or four times as heavy as the next. Strength tends to go with weight, but even a heavy piece of wood can be brittle if the grain is bad. For a main wing spar, strong, springy wood should be used. Soft and brittle material may be saved for somewhere less vital. The colour and texture of the wood gives some clues and a quick check weighing with a letter balance can be very informative.

This end usable   Warp here

Strip wood

Straight grain preferable   Short grain, weak, best not used

Thin edge   Damaged edge   Split

Knot   Deep saw marks   Packing marks   Crushed

Sheet wood

Quarter grained wood. Stiff but may be brittle. Used for wing ribs but not for sheet covering of curved surfaces

Figure 8.1 *Some possible defects of timber in model building.*

If the kit contains some heavy and some light wood for the wing, try to balance the two sides so that all the heavy stuff is not on one and all the light on the other. If some of the ribs appear noticeably stiffer than others, sort them out for use in the central parts of the wing and save the light ones for the outer panels. Light material is best for the tail unit, for reasons connected with balance.

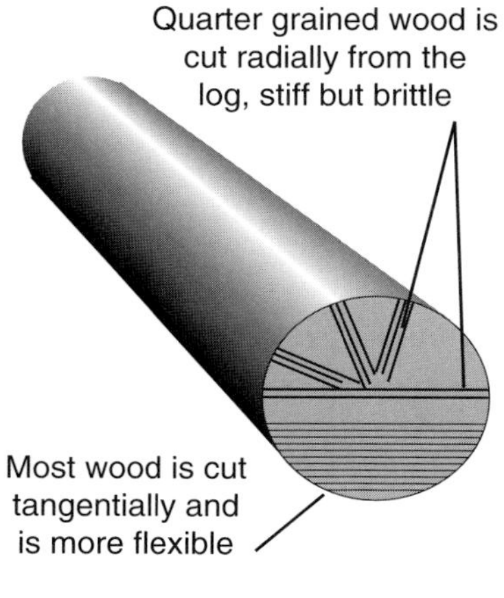

Two pieces of wood may vary in stiffness even though they are similar in weight. If a piece of sheet balsa is to be used to cover part of the wing it will have to curve to follow the shape of the ribs. This piece needs to be flexible in the direction of the bend. If it has a speckled and figured appearance because it has been cut on the **quarter grain** it may be too stiff (Fig. 8.2). On the other hand, such quarter grain wood can be used to make stiff wing ribs and fuselage cross formers.

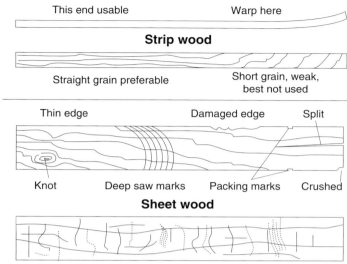

Quarter grained wood is cut radially from the log, stiff but brittle

Most wood is cut tangentially and is more flexible

Figure 8.2 *Quarter and tangentially sawn wood.*

HANDLING THE TOOLS

The knife blade should be sharp. Replace it when it shows signs of making ragged cuts. It is a mistake to think that blunt knives and other tools are safe. They are more dangerous than sharp instruments because they require more force to be applied when cutting. A small slip then can cause a serious injury. A sharp blade will cut with little effort and is less likely to slip. An old but still valid rule is; **keep the hands** (and fingers) always **behind the cutting edge**.

There is a wide range of small modelling knives, with replaceable blades, on the market, which are good for fine work. The type of craft knife that allows the blunt tip to be snapped off, exposing a fresh edge, is very convenient, though not suitable for all work. Occasionally such a blade will snap unexpectedly, which can be dangerous. The clip-on blades used on surgical scalpels are not entirely satisfactory for modelling, since they too can snap when under pressure. Single edged razor blades may be useful sometimes.

When cutting or carving wood, take note of the grain direction and avoid running the cut in such a way that the grain encourages the blade to slice away from the line, spoiling the part being cut out. Use a metal ruler or straight edge to guide the knife whenever possible. When cutting through thicknesses more than two or three millimetres, make a light cut on one side and then turn the wood over and cut from the other side in the same place, rather than trying to go right through in one heavy stroke. When cutting across grain, even a sharp knife tends to crush the wood. It is better to use a fine saw (razor saw) on thicknesses more than 3mm. Cut outside the line, rather than exactly on it, or the piece will come out slightly too small.

ABRASIVE PAPER

Abrasive papers (sand paper, glass paper, carborundum paper, garnet paper, wet and dry papers, etc.) are among the most necessary and useful tools for model aircraft building. Coarse papers can be used to shape blocks and thick sheets of wood, fine and very fine papers are needed for finishing and for smoothing prior to covering and/or painting.

The paper should be mounted on a **sanding block**. Suitable blocks can be bought but any conveniently shaped and sized piece of wood or metal that comes to hand, will do. The paper may be folded round the block and pinned or taped on, or glued on with contact adhesive. **Aluminium T-bar** sections can make excellent sanding blocks if a few offcuts of this metal are available.

Holding the paper in the hand without a block causes an uneven result, exaggerating rather than removing any imperfections. For curved shapes, the paper may be mounted on a piece of old broom handle or round wooden dowelling, or a special small block may be shaped for a particular task.

The paper is a cutting tool and should be 'sharp'. When a piece is worn, replace it with fresh. Stripping it off the block is easy even if it has been glued on. Very worn papers can be useful sometimes for rubbing down paintwork.

RAZOR PLANES

Model and craft shops sell razor planes, which, as the name suggests, have the old-fashioned type of two-edged razor blade mounted with one edge protruding slightly through the mouth in the sole of the plane. These are very useful for shaping wing leading edges and for other light planing work. The blade requires careful adjustment to produce a thin shaving of wood. The blades must be replaced when blunt.

USING THE PLANS

Read all the instructions and study the plans attentively. Work out the building procedure step by step before starting. Even experts are sometimes caught out by assembling things in the wrong order, which may mean having to undo or scrap work that has been completed in order to get some vital part into its place. It should not be necessary to change the design in any way but occasionally an obvious fault or weakness may be improved. Experienced advice is very helpful here.

The plan is spread out flat on the building board and may be taped down. It should be protected by laying a sheet of transparent polythene over it, or at least rubbed with the end of a wax candle, to prevent glue from sticking to it. If taken care of in this way the plan may be used again to build further models, or to help with repairs.

The wing and other components are assembled on the flat board over the plan, pins or small weights being used to hold the various parts in their correct positions. Assemble the parts dry, without glue, in the first place, to check that they fit correctly and that nothing has been lost. Anything that seems to require heavy pressure to make it slot into place, or fails to fit the space for it, should be checked to see that it is going into the right part of the model. If it still seems unduly tight, ease the joint gently with a file or knife until it fits without heavy pressure. Sloppy fits are not desirable, but a good joint does not need forcing either.

If some small piece of the kit has been lost or broken before assembly, it may be repaired or replaced by cutting a replacement for it from wood of the same weight and thickness.

PINNING DOWN

When pinning things down before gluing it is best not to drive the pin through spars or longerons, since this weakens them. Use plenty of pins but whenever possible place them on either side of the member to be held, angling the pins in such a way that they keep the item in its place. Avoid crushing the wood. The pins are to hold things in position while the glue sets, no more. Larger pieces, blocks and wide sheets of wood, may safely be pinned through.

Be ready if necessary to pack the leading edge up to the correct height above the board to make accurate junction with the wing ribs. This can be done with small pieces of waste wood. Make sure that the ribs and spars slot fully home before leaving them to dry after gluing.

GLUES

As mentioned earlier, ordinary **white** PVA **wood glue** is very good for most of the construction of a model glider and can be used exclusively, except for metal parts. The PVA takes a little time to set but it gives a strong, slightly flexible joint which is ideal. It is also able to creep into and fill small gaps. This glue is almost transparent when dry. It is not fully waterproof, which is not a serious problem for gliders unless the model is left out too long in the rain or, of course, is allowed to fall into a river, lake, or the sea. Cleaning up after using this adhesive is also easy with soap and water. In tight corners, the glue can be applied on the end of a toothpick. As the work proceeds, wipe or scrape away, with a small scrap of wood or cloth, any surplus glue from the joint. This saves weight and helps drying.

PVA glue takes a while to 'grab' the wood, and a few hours to set fully. People in a hurry look for quicker setting adhesives.

Another minor problem is that the PVA never does go completely hard, so if it is necessary to smooth over a joint by sanding it the glue tends to wriggle to and fro under the abrasive block, instead of being rubbed down. This rarely matters for the internal structure of a model. The slight flexibility is a good feature because joints tend to spring under load instead of snapping, but may be a nuisance with joints on the outside where sheet balsa skins are joined, or along the leading edge of the wing, which should be smoothly sanded to a round section.

PVA is not the best glue to use when a large area of wood has to be stuck, as when a plywood doubler has to be glued to a balsa fuselage side. The water in the glue expands the wood and causes it to develop a curl when drying (contact adhesive is better here; see below).

A glue which is similar in most respects to PVA is **aliphatic resin glue**. This has most of the same properties but sets harder and sands down more readily; however, not all model shops stock it.

Epoxy resin glues, involving the mixing of hardener and resin, are excellent for gluing metal parts, such as wing joiner tubes, to wood. Mixing thoroughly is very important. There are two main varieties. The so-called five- or six-minute epoxy glue takes an initial set in a few minutes, depending on the temperature. Many model fliers carry quick setting epoxy to the flying field with them, to make small repairs quickly.

The slow setting epoxy requires much longer curing time, and is somewhat stronger. Both types are heavy and expensive, but are used in very small amounts. It is a mistake to think that pouring large amounts of this glue onto and around a joint, makes it stronger. Use only enough to make the junction, and wipe away the surplus.

Apart from glue, epoxy resins of more liquid type have many uses, such as laminating glass cloth and sticking veneers to foam-cored wings. The beginner is not likely to need these materials at first.

A very few people are **allergic to epoxy materials** and may have trouble with breathing in a bad case. No-one should work in badly ventilated spaces and **barrier creams** and **gloves** should be worn. **Acetone** is useful for cleaning up, but once fully cured it is impossible to remove epoxy glues from clothing or carpets.

Polyester resins set faster than epoxy and are often employed to reinforce fuselages with layers of glass cloth. A very small amount of the catalyst is mixed with the resin and it begins to set or 'cure' almost immediately. After curing there is a waxy exterior which needs to be cleaned off before painting.

If too much polyester is mixed at a time in a deep mixing vessel, it becomes very hot and cures itself rock hard in a few moments. Mix only enough for the next few minutes' work.

Take great care with the **catalyst**. Very serious injury to the **eyes** can be caused if this material is handled carelessly.

Contact adhesives are useful for making joints where it is difficult to clamp or pin the wood together. An example is when a large piece of sheet balsa is used to skin over a built-up framework. Another case is the gluing together of a sheet of balsa and a plywood doubler. The glue is spread where required on both the pieces to be joined, and, after a short time, the parts are brought together and pressed down to give immediate adhesion. Once together, the parts cannot be separated so it is important to make the initial contact accurately.

A large range of **cyanoacrylate** or CA glues have become available in recent times. Sold under names like *Hot Stuff* and *Zap*, these are the modeller's equivalent of the so-called superglue obtainable from hardware shops, and will stick almost anything to anything else. The model shops sell CA glues in larger bottles at much lower prices, although the price of a relatively small bottle of the glue is still high.

The more liquid varieties of these glues take only a few seconds to set. Instead of applying glue to a joint and then bringing the two parts together, the technique is to assemble the joint carefully, dry, and then apply a droplet of the glue. The liquid instantly soaks into the joint, which must be a good fit, and hardens. A very small drop spreads a long way and sets in less time than it takes to tell. Naturally, if the joint was not correctly lined up, it cannot be undone afterwards. CA glue is very hard when set. There is no slight flexibility as there is with PVA wood glue. The wood breaks before the glue yields.

There are disadvantages apart from the price. If the joint is not a close fit, the liquid glue will not fill any gap. It forms a hard shell on the surface of the wood and it then becomes quite difficult to make a joint there at all. Applying extra liquid glue to a bad joint that has not 'taken' the first time, will not help.

Some of these glues get quite hot when hardening, producing a rather acrid smoke which is said not to be harmful. More recently, this minor difficulty has been overcome and the newer types of superglues do not smoke or smell.

It is particularly dangerous to get CA *glue into the eyes.*

When the fingers get stuck together, which does happen, it is easy to peel them apart gradually when merely forcing them would remove skin. For more serious mistakes with this glue, solvents are available.

The thicker type of CA glue takes longer to set. Because it does not soak into the wood so easily it will fill small gaps and it hardens in less than a minute. Small bottles of **accelerator** are available, with a spray nozzle, for setting this CA glue even more quickly. This has become the standard adhesive for many modellers for almost all construction work and for making rapid repairs on the flying field. The solid glue is extremely hard when set and almost impossible to sand down or cut.

With some of the most common brands of CA glue, the pinhole-sized nozzle tends to get clogged up. By holding the bottle upright and squeezing it slightly, before putting it down, the drop of glue in the nozzle can be expelled, leav-

ing the hole open. Glue should then be ready to flow through next time.

CA glues should not be stored in a hot place or left lying in the sun. When warm, shelf life is not very long. A neglected bottle will begin to thicken, become stringy and solidify eventually. To store the glue longer, some people keep the unopened bottles in a refrigerator, clearly labelled.

Balsa cement, which once was the only glue suitable for balsa wood, is now rarely used, though it is still available. It is useful for edge-to-edge jointing of long and wide balsa sheets, but the beginner is not likely to need to do this with the first one or two models. **PVC glues** for assembling plastic model kits are quite **unsuitable** for wood.

There are many other adhesives available nowadays, all of which may find some application in modelling at some time. The common ones have been mentioned above.

MATING THE WINGS

If the two half wings are built separately, one fairly common mistake is to set the joining rods

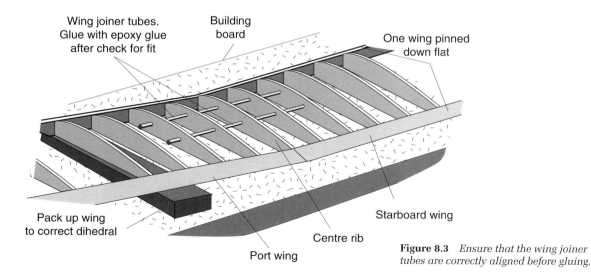

Figure 8.3 *Ensure that the wing joiner tubes are correctly aligned before gluing.*

Wing joiner tubes. Glue with epoxy glue after check for fit

Building board

One wing pinned down flat

Pack up wing to correct dihedral

Port wing

Centre rib

Starboard wing

and tubes slightly out of position, so when the wing is assembled the two halves do not mate correctly. In a bad case it may even prove impossible to get the wing joiner rods to line up with their tubes at all. It helps if the final gluing of the joiners is postponed until both wings can be set up on the building board accurately butted together as they will be in flight, with the tubes and rods in place (Fig. 8.3).

The joiners are then adjusted for good fit and the tubes glued in place so that alignment is assured (Fig. 8.4). Packing and blocking may be needed to get the correct dihedral angle. If the wing has some sheet wood covering at the root, this should be left off until the tubes are in place.

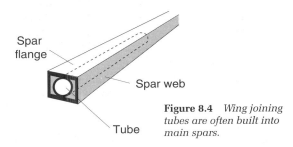

Figure 8.4 *Wing joining tubes are often built into main spars.*

AVOIDING WARPS IN WING AND TAIL

It is important that the wing and tail should be built without any twist. This is why the flatness of the building board on which the parts are

assembled and pinned while gluing, is so important, but even with a perfectly flat building surface, sometimes when the assembled part is unpinned from the flat board it immediately springs out of line. There are several causes for this. One is the inevitable slight bowing or warping that all wood is prone to. There is no way of preventing this entirely – even laying a piece of wood down on the shelf one way up rather than the other or leaning it against a wall for a few days or weeks, can introduce a bow or twist. Examine each strip before pinning down. Various ways can be tried to straighten any bad bow. One is to dampen the wood and pin it down to dry straight. If a small amount of **liquid ammonia** is added to the water, this makes the process even easier. Another dodge is to sandpaper the curved wood gently along the outer side of the bow. This contracts the wood fibres a little on that side and can straighten the curve or even reverse it. Even a gentle rubbing with the fingers can sometimes have this effect. For the same reason, avoid sanding or rubbing strips of wood on one side only; this can create a bow where there was none.

Another cause of warping is failure to check the fit of the various parts before gluing. Wedging an undersized slot in a rib or former down

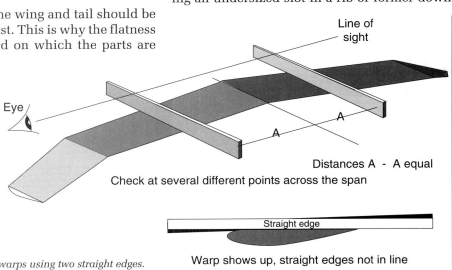

Figure 8.5 *Checking for warps using two straight edges.*

hard onto a spar will distort the structure. The assembly should not be pulled out of shape to bring loose joints together. A really sloppy fit can be made good by gluing in a scrap of wood to pack it out and this should be done if necessary. It is better carefully to pack a loose joint than to force a tight one.

Another hint is to delay removing the newly completed framework of the wing from the building board for a few days. This not only ensures the glue will harden fully, but allows the timber to settle down into its final shape and it will tend to stay flat afterwards.

Twists in a finished wing can be detected by careful inspection. If there is some doubt, winding strips should be used (Fig. 8.5). Lay two straight strips of wood, or two rulers, chordwise across the wing on the underside, and sight them from the tip. If there is a warp the strips will not be in line with one another.

If the wing is deliberately built with some washout, the winding strips will show this, so what needs to be checked then is that left and right wings have the correct twist and both the same direction. Both wings should be alike!

WARPS CAUSED BY COVERING

Covering a light wooden framework such as a wing or, even more, a tailplane, may introduce warps that were not there in the framework. The tension of the covering as it is shrunk is high and sometimes it is impossible to prevent a warp developing.

CORRECTING WARPS

Fortunately, if an unwanted warp does appear in a film- or fabric-covered wing, it is usually easy to correct it by applying gentle heat and twisting the wing by hand back to its correct shape or slightly beyond, holding it as it cools for a little time to let the tension equalise. On cooling, the result should be checked and, if not quite right, a little further warmth and corrective pressure should produce the right outcome. An electric radiator gives more than enough heat for this, though specialised heat guns, similar in principle to electric hair driers, are available both to shrink the covering in the first place, and to adjust warps.

WARPS IN FOAM-CORED WINGS

With a foam-cored wing warping is less likely but it can occur and correction is more difficult. Such wings are very stiff, which is one of the advantages of this structure. Depending on the adhesive used in the veneering operation, careful warming of the wing to soften the glue may enable a correction to be made. Seek help from an experienced model builder.

Bends in the wing in the spanwise direction, causing a slight bowing as distinct from a twist, are less important, but should be avoided if possible.

Even after the model is completed and has done some flying, warps may be introduced if the wings are left lying about carelessly. If they are to be left idle for some time they should be kept flat.

FUSELAGES THAT TWIST

Any formers used to support the fuselage sides should be checked for accuracy with a carpenter's try square. As the assembly takes shape, further checks of squareness should be done at every step.

Fuselages often become distorted if the two sides are not matched. They should be checked against one another and trued up before assembly. The plans will probably indicate that the fuselage sides should bend slightly inwards. If the timber on one side is markedly stiffer than the other, when making the bends the stiffer wood will resist as the other yields and the result will be very disappointing. The timber on both sides should therefore be matched in weight and stiffness. If there are plywood doublers the ply too should be examined to see if it has a slight curvature already. If it has, try to use this to advantage, matching the two sides to curve towards one another, rather than pulling in a way that will introduce an asymmetrical shape.

PREFORMING WOOD

The best answer to making curved members and preventing warps in fuselages is to preform the wood by steaming it or soaking it in hot water, with a little ammonia. Balsa wood when wet becomes extremely easy to manipulate and can be weighted or pinned down on a form to take up almost any desired curve after drying. Plywood, pine and spruce are less malleable but the same applies – they can be made to take up a curve after wetting or steaming to soften the fibres. Some patience is needed to let the wood dry thoroughly before using it (the glue used in plywood should be waterproof but light dampening will not penetrate to the glue line).

HINGES AND HORNS

The model kit may provide hinges for the control surfaces, with instructions for fitting them. If not, hinges are bought separately.

Probably the best all round hinge for the beginner is flexible Mylar plastic, which can be cut up as needed into pieces about the size of postage stamps (Fig. 8.6). The Mylar may be roughened slightly with abrasive paper. The modelling knife is used then to cut slits in the control surfaces and the members they are to attach to, and the small hinge strips are slid into place. It is very important to fasten the hinges securely, but not so securely that they will not work at all. Various ways of doing this are used. One way relies on thin cyanoacrylate glue. After slipping the Mylar into place, a little CA is applied to soak into the slits and is considered sufficient. This can be done after the model has been covered.

If CA glue is not used, PVA or epoxy will do, but then a fine drill should be used to make a hole right through the wood and Mylar, and a small peg, perhaps made from a toothpick, driven through and glued to hold the hinge in place, smoothing the ends down afterwards by careful sanding. The main snag with this is that

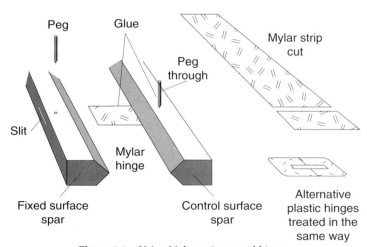

Figure 8.6 *Using Mylar strip control hinges.*

if the fixing and pegging of the hinges is done after covering the model, the covering will be damaged. Fixing the hinges before covering makes the job of applying the covering more difficult.

A popular form of plastic hinge now available is similar in principle to the Mylar strip but has a slightly 'hairy' finish and a slot which encourages the glue to soak into the joint when the hinge is fitted. These are bought separately ready for use and may be included in the kit. Pinning through is not usually necessary.

Other types of hinge require greater care to ensure that glue does not get into them and prevent their easy operation.

Control horns for the first model will normally be of nylon and should come with the bolts or screws needed to mount them correctly on elevator and rudder (Fig. 8.7). They need to be positioned correctly to make it easy to attach the control rod linkages, which the model plan should show clearly. Before fitting the horns, check with the pushrods and the servo movements, to ensure that the control will work the proper way with the transmitter sticks – left rudder, left stick, up elevator, back stick etc.

COVERING AND COLOURING

Assuming that plastic film will be used for the first model or two, the instructions given with the roll of material should be followed exactly. The covering film itself is quite costly. The cheapest is not always the best, so if there is any doubt, seek advice on this point.

It is natural to want the model to look attractive and, if the fuselage is painted, it can be coloured in some way that harmonises with the wings and tail. Special paints can be bought to match some of the plastic films on the market. Some films are transparent, which makes the model light up vividly in the sun. The temptation to make the first model too beautiful should be resisted, however. Applying a fine finish takes a lot of time and energy and the first model will surely be damaged before long. It becomes disheartening if many hours have been spent in rubbing down and painting, to see cracks, dents and patches appearing. In the first instance, a good working finish is all that is required and plastic film all over will achieve this.

Choice of colours needs a little thought. One of the problems every radio control pilot has is

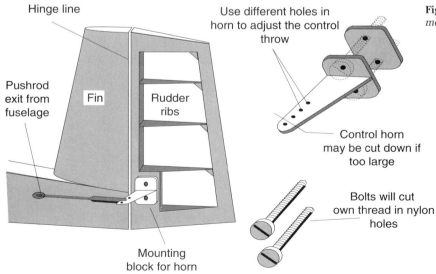

Hinge line

Use different holes in horn to adjust the control throw

Pushrod exit from fuselage

Fin

Rudder ribs

Control horn may be cut down if too large

Bolts will cut own thread in nylon holes

Mounting block for horn

Figure 8.7 *Typical arrangement of control horn on rudder.*

recognising the position of the model in the air. It is very easy indeed to become disoriented, to think the model is flying towards you when it is actually going away, to believe it is turning right when it is really going round to the left. The choice of colours can help.

In almost all conditions, dark and opaque colours show up better against the sky than light shades. Avoid light grey or polished silver, light yellow, pale blue and other pastel shades. Pure white shows up well under a blue sky but in some conditions can almost vanish against clouds. Dark red and green, deep yellow, orange, black and midnight blue, show up well.

It is good to have two contrasting colours. A very dark shade may be used on the underside of the wings and tail and perhaps the fuselage, and a different, brighter colour on top. The wing outer panels may be one colour, the inner sections different. Then, as the model turns this way and that in the distance, the colours seem almost to flash on and off, giving the pilot a good indication of what the model is doing. Another

idea is to have one wing, or the outer part of it, different from the other, so again, there is an indication to the ground of which way the model is flying. On the fin or the nose, a single piece of highly polished metal foil will catch the light and flash like a mirror in certain positions.

Too many different colours on a model do not help. If the general outline is broken up into a number of patches, the result is a sort of dazzle effect, similar to camouflage, even if the individual colours are bright.

In devising a colour scheme, think in darkish shades for the lower surfaces and adopt a very simple pattern that will emphasise, rather than obscure, the outline of the glider. When experience has been gained and the orientation problem is not so severe (it never goes away entirely), more adventurous colours can be tried.

Later models may use composite materials and resins that are affected by heat from the sun. These may require at least the upper surfaces to be white to avoid heat absorption.

chapter nine

FITTING THE RADIO INTO THE MODEL

THE BATTERY BOX

Near the nose of the model there will be a space for the battery, which is the heaviest single item (Fig. 9.1). Different sizes of battery are used but the most likely is a 600 milliamp-hour type which will consist of four cells arranged in a rectangular pack, about 60mm (2.4in.) long, and 30mm (1.2in.) square. The battery compartment is sure to receive a lot of heavy hammering from the inside, so may be lined with plywood. An additional internal skin of glass cloth and resin is often recommended too. The battery should not be allowed to slide about inside its box. If it can move too freely, in any but the gentlest of landings it becomes a little battering ram and bursts the fuselage open. It may be restrained with small pieces of plastic packing material like that in which the radio control gear comes, or something similar. This firm material is better

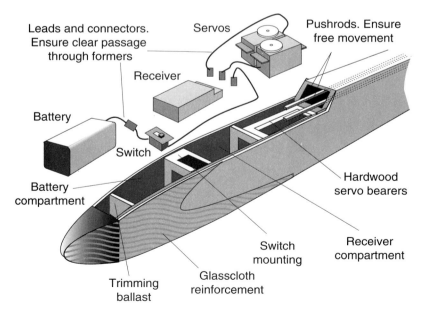

Leads and connectors. Ensure clear passage through formers

Servos

Pushrods. Ensure free movement

Receiver

Battery

Switch

Battery compartment

Trimming ballast

Glasscloth reinforcement

Switch mounting

Receiver compartment

Hardwood servo bearers

Figure 9.1 *General layout of radio equipment in the model. There is not much room to spare. Servos must be screwed securely to hardwood bearers or plywood tray. The switch may be mounted by cutting a small hole in the fuselage side to allow access from outside.*

than sponge rubber which spreads out sideways under a shock and can burst the fuselage almost as readily as an unrestrained battery. Ensure also that the battery cannot jump up out of its compartment if the glider flies in rough air or even turns upside down.

Make sure that there is space for the wires. If the leads have to be compressed or dragged every time the battery is removed or replaced, they can be broken and even short circuited, which destroys the battery. If dry batteries are used they should be taped or banded into place to prevent being shaken loose.

THE RECEIVER COMPARTMENT

The receiver is usually fitted immediately behind the battery and it is best to protect it all round with some sponge rubber packing. The idea is partly to protect the radio from direct shocks in crashes, but a more serious danger comes from the rather heavy servos which, if mounted behind the receiver, can, in a bad crash, break from their mountings and charge forward to smash into whatever is in the way. It is probably safer to have the servos in front with the receiver behind them, but in this position it may interfere with the control pushrods.

Whether the receiver is behind or in front of the servos, provision must be made for the aerial. It may be run inside the fuselage. Some people use a row of drinking straws end to end, or a plastic tube, as a conduit. If this is to be done the tube is best glued onto the fuselage floor or one of its sides before closing up the long, narrow tail end.

As mentioned earlier there may be some loss of operating range with an internal aerial – an external aerial is safer. The rather fine aerial wire has to be passed through an exit hole in the fuselage. The edges of the hole may cause wear to the insulation, so a small rubber grommet should be used to protect it. After exiting, the aerial may be taped to the side of the fuselage,

or perhaps suspended to an attachment point on the top of the fin. It is not necessary to stretch the aerial tightly but it is important that it should not be bunched up. It is true that an external aerial creates some extra air drag in flight, but better this than having the glider go out of range.

SERVO MOUNTINGS

The servos have to be mounted firmly, since they must not wobble to and fro as the control loads come onto them through the pushrods. Nor should they break loose in an average bad landing.

The servo bearers or tray should not be of balsa wood but hardwood or plywood, tough enough to take screws and hold them firmly despite many knocks. Balsa plywood, provided in some kits, is not really quite good enough for this. A 3mm plywood tray may be made, or servo bearers, 6mm (¼ in.) square, may be cut to run across the fuselage, where the ends should be glued and supported firmly (plastic trays are sometimes included with the radio but these rarely seem to fit neatly into a glider).

Each servo is provided with four small rubber **grommets** and is held down by screws through these. The screw head requires a washer to prevent it pulling itself right through the rubber. Then the grommet should be compressed enough so that it spreads out to hold the servo, but not crushed beyond all flexibility. The servo should be firm in its seating without being totally rigid.

The drive arms or wheels on the servos can be taken off and repositioned as needed. Several different kinds of drive arm are provided and the modeller chooses whatever suits best. Unwanted bits of drive arm can be cut off. The arm will have several holes. The pushrod end is clipped into the drive arm at a point which gives the amount of control movement required, with a similar adjustment available at the control horn.

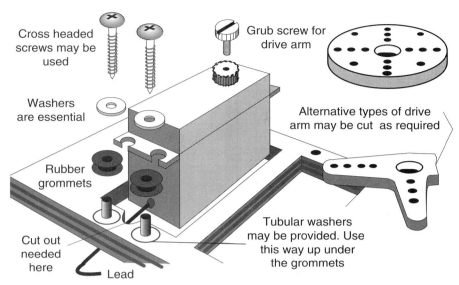

Cross headed screws may be used

Grub screw for drive arm

Washers are essential

Alternative types of drive arm may be cut as required

Rubber grommets

Cut out needed here

Lead

Tubular washers may be provided. Use this way up under the grommets

Servos must be securely mounted, preferably on hardwood bearers or plywood tray. Screwing into soft balsa wood is not sufficient

Figure 9.2 *A typical servo assembly.*

When two servos are close together there must be enough room to allow full movement of the controls and pushrods at all times. This should be checked before making the installation. The longer drive arms may have to be cut to help with problems of clearance, and the holes in them may require easing very slightly to take the pushrod ends.

Servos may be mounted in any position and will still work perfectly (Fig. 9.2). They can, for instance, be fitted side by side, one behind the other, upside down, sideways, or crossways relative to the fuselage, or at some angle. For easy access to connect the pushrods to them and to make adjustments, the simplest possible, upright servo mounting is usually the best but if another position is better, it should be adopted.

In a heavy crash, the **servo gears** may be damaged without any external sign of it. Several teeth may be stripped off one or more of the tiny wheels. The control may appear to operate fairly well but haltingly or with movement restricted in one direction. In a bad case the servo will chatter wildly or run out of control. Getting a new set of gears is a normal part of the model shop service and should not be too costly. The shop will also do the repair, for a small fee, but the modeller can replace a broken gear wheel by removing the drive arm and then unscrewing the servo case, usually held with four small bolts. The top of the case then comes off, with a little persuasion. Take care because the gears tend to fall out and may be lost. Try to keep the wheels and their little spindles in place so that they can be put back together in the correct order easily. If the positions are lost, there is only one correct way of reassembling the gear train so take this slowly and work out how it has to be done. Find which gear wheel, or wheels, have been stripped, clean out any scraps of broken teeth, and replace the damaged wheels with new. Keep any spare old gear wheels if they are in good shape. They might be needed for another replacement.

If for any reason the servo motor or the electronic components in the lower part of the case are damaged and not working, it is usually not worth trying to get them repaired. A new servo will almost certainly be necessary.

Like any mechanical thing, servos require servicing from time to time. If there is any doubt the servo should be checked and, if necessary, replaced before flying.

CONTROL THROWS

The model plan should state the control movements. If not, it is enough, for a first model, to have about 20 degrees of total movement on the elevator, 10 up and 10 down, and up to 50 degrees, 25 left, 25 right, on the rudder. After some experience, both may be changed to suit the pilot. Providing there is adequate movement, the matter is not critical.

The elevator sensitivity depends greatly on the centre of gravity position. Elevators are often too sensitive for the beginner. Although decreasing the movement will help, it is more effective to add some ballast to the nose of the glider, to move the centre of gravity forward (see Chapter 10 *Balancing the model*).

The effectiveness of the rudder, on a beginner's model, depends chiefly on the dihedral angle of the wing. If the rudder is not effective enough with the 25 degrees suggested, it will not be much improved by increasing the movement. What is probably required is an increase in the dihedral angle of the wing (see Chapter 12 *How the glider controls work*). Such an increase can often be achieved very simply by bending the wing joiner rods to a larger angle, but if the wing is not of this type, some reconstruction may have to be done.

THE BITS AND PIECES

When planning the radio layout in the model, do not forget that the **switch** and its **harness of wires, plugs**, etc., take up quite a lot of space. There have to be ways through for the wires to link battery, switch, receiver and servos all together. This may require some cutting of holes in fuselage cross formers, **before** they are assembled. For instance, if the battery plug is of a certain size and the switch is on the other side of a former, a hole in the former, big enough to let the plug pass through, is needed.

The wires should be sorted out as neatly as possible and tucked away so that they do not foul the controls and are not under any strain. With a nicad battery it will also be necessary to arrange for plugging into the charger. To have wires or a charge connector flopping about near the servo drive arm where they can jam something, is asking for trouble. A little forethought will avoid this. Remember also that everything may need to come out again to be fitted into another model.

The switch may be mounted so that it can be operated from outside the fuselage. This entails cutting a small hole in the fuselage for the switch to protrude, and bolting it in place. As mentioned earlier, this is not always a good idea since the switch can be knocked on or off too easily. It can be mounted more safely inside. To remind the pilot to switch on before launching, the hatch can be left open always when the model is on the ground. Switching on and replacing the hatch then becomes automatic. But do not forget to switch off after landing, to save the battery!

CONTROL RODS

The simplest kind of pushrod to link the servo drive arm to the control horn of the rudder or elevator, is a length of stiff wood, balsa or harder wood dowel with a piece of stiff wire attached, glued and bound at each end (Fig. 9.3). The actual strength of the rod is not so important as its stiffness. When the controls come under load, a flexible rod can suddenly bow, so that no

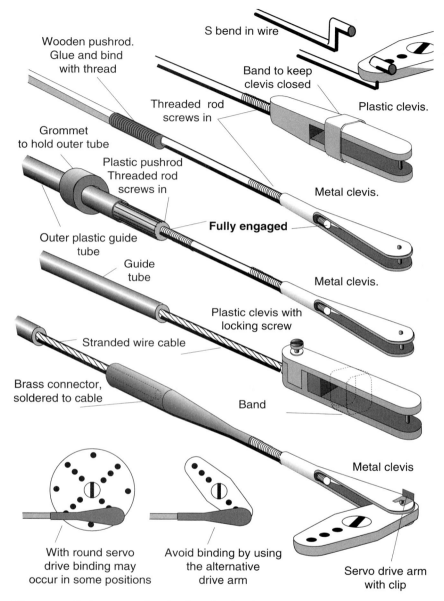

S bend in wire

Wooden pushrod.
Glue and bind
with thread

Band to keep
clevis closed

Threaded rod
screws in

Plastic clevis.

Grommet
to hold outer tube

Plastic pushrod
Threaded rod
screws in

Metal clevis.

Fully engaged

Outer plastic guide
tube

Guide
tube

Metal clevis.

Plastic clevis with
locking screw

Stranded wire cable

Brass connector,
soldered to cable

Band

Metal clevis

With round servo
drive binding may
occur in some positions

Avoid binding by using
the alternative
drive arm

Servo drive arm
with clip

Figure 9.3 *Various types of pushrod, pushrod ends and clevis attachments to the servo arm may be used. All are satisfactory if fitted in accordance with maker's instructions.*

control action occurs. Aluminium tubing is light and stiff, or on large models expensive arrow shafts may be used instead of wood, for the rods. In all cases, the rods must run straight and should not rub against the internal structure of the fuselage. Nor should the elevator and rudder control rods rub against one another in any possible position of the controls in flight. Where the wire at the end of a wooden pushrod rod has to protrude through a slot in the rear fuselage, it is almost sure to rub against the sides of the slot. This cannot be helped but the friction is not usually enough to be a serious nuisance. Plastic slot guides can be bought to help here.

One way of attaching a drive rod to a control horn, is to bend the wire to an S shape at the end and push this through the hole in the horn. Although this can be satisfactory it does involve some force and this may enlarge the hole, making for a slightly sloppy fit and hence a wobbly control surface. This may not be serious for the beginner but it is not desirable.

Wooden pushrods take up space in the narrow fuselage and for this reason most people use the various kinds of plastic-sheathed control rods that are available. These take up less space and have a certain amount of flexibility. There is normally a plastic guide tube which should be glued firmly in place at each end and at several points along the length as well. The guide should not be bent or curved more than absolutely necessary, certainly never kinked sharply. The actual pushrod, which may also be plastic or possibly a steel wire or cable, then slides inside the guide freely.

At least one end of the rod should be capable of adjustment in length, so the wire end is threaded to take an adjustable link or clevis. People have sometimes used bicycle spokes for the pushrod end but the thread may not fit the clevis connectors and there is not much thread on the spoke for adjustment. More suitable threaded wire is usually supplied with the clevises. Make sure the clevis and the rod do fit. The threads from different manufacturers do not always match.

Often both ends of the control rod will be threaded with a clevis at each end, which gives more possibility of adjustment. It is possible, in this case, for the rod to disconnect itself gradually by turning round and round inside the

guide, one end working up and the other end unscrewing until it falls off. Lock nuts are provided but are not entirely reliable. After the first few coarse adjustments have been made, it is wise to lock one of the clevises with a dab of glue. Adjustments can still be made at the other end. A clevis should never be unscrewed so far that the thread on the rod is not fully engaged.

The clevis, once in place, should be locked to the control horn or servo drive, either with a small plastic band or with the metal clip provided. It is not very likely that an unlocked clevis will fall off but the locking band or clip is a good precaution.

Instead of the clevis ends for pushrods, ball and socket linkages are sometimes used. These are especially valuable where a control rod approaches the servo drive arm at an unusual angle, or when, as the control moves, the angle changes to some extent. The ball end allows the drive rod to move smoothly through a fair range of angles. For the ordinary model this is not likely to be needed but if at some time spoilers, dive brakes or ailerons are fitted, ball and socket linkages may be appropriate.

A type of control arrangement sometimes seen, mostly for rudders, is the closed loop, which relies on lengths of fine cable (such as fisherman's trace line) or Kevlar fibre thread, making a continuous loop from one side of the drive arm, to a horn on one side of the rudder and back from the horn on the other side of the rudder to the servo drive arm. In the case of an elevator, the line may pass round a small pulley to complete the loop, the horn being attached on the way. This system resembles that used on older types of full-sized gliders and aeroplanes. The advantage of using Kevlar rather than steel wires or cables is said to be that the fibre causes no radio interference, while wires or cables might do so. In fact such a problem rarely arises, especially if the receiver aerial is externally mounted.

The kit out of the box. Ask to see this before buying. Check the quality of the wood and the die cutting of parts which should not require sawing. In this case they are excellent, coming out with very little effort as shown. There are sealed plastic bags for the small items such as hinges, control horns etc. Look at the plan and the instructions. A rolled plan rather than a folded one is preferred because it will lie flat without creases.

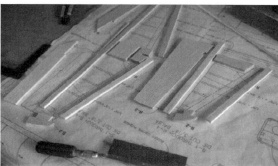

I began with the tail unit. The parts were located in the kit and, where necessary, separated out from their die cut sheets. The leading and trailing edges had to be cut to size with the small saw and the knife. The rudder and elevators required careful sanding to bring the trailing edges to a near knife edge. I used a sanding block for this and took time with it.

The parts were then pinned down on the building board and glued together over the plan, which was protected with a sheet of transparent polythene. Aligning the elevator halves on the hard wood dowel required a little care. A small piece of glass cloth can be used here to strengthen the glued joint.

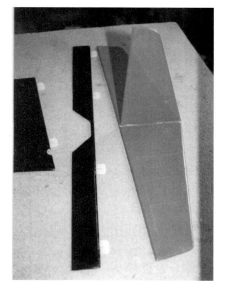

The tail unit is best covered before final assembly. However, areas where gluing will be required must be left clear of the plastic film. That is, a narrow strip where the fin is to be on the tailplane, and a small area underneath where the tailplane is glued to the rear of the fuselage. The hinges are shown here glued into their slits in the elevator and rudder. They were then slipped into corresponding slits in the fixed tail and held with a drop of CA glue.

The fuselage sides, already cut to shape in balsa plywood when the kit was opened, were pinned down flat on the plan. The longerons were glued in place exactly along the edges. It is most important not to make two right-hand or two left-hand sides. This is avoided by laying them side by side with the bottom edges adjoining, but don't glue them together by accident!

The formers, easily separated from their cut sheets, after gentle sanding are ready for gluing in place. The largest one here being checked for position and fit. Note the holes at each side of this former to allow the pushrods to go through to the tail. The central large hole is only to reduce weight slightly, the small round hole will take the small dowel for the wing holding bands.

The fuselage was assembled, taking care that everything was square and that the assembly fitted over the plan. The formers were glued, the pushrod guides fed through their holes which had to be enlarged slightly. They were glued firmly at both ends and at several places in between. The floor of the fuselage was planked, the top planking and nose block came next.

It is easy to get a banana-shaped fuselage, or to build in a twist, so check and check again before gluing. If the two fuselage sides tend to warp it may be necessary to damp them to soften the wood and then pin or clamp them to pull them into line, and let them dry before finally gluing them.

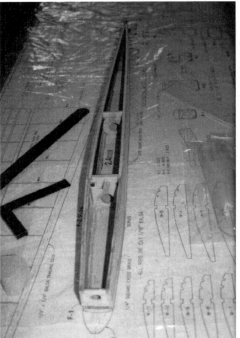

A close-up view of the rubber band retaining dowel and the pushrod guides.

Assembling the centre section of the wing. The ribs were eas-ily separated from their cut sheets. The lower flange of the main spar was pinned down, over the protected plan, with-out driving any pins through the wood. The ribs themselves were then used to position the leading and trailing edge mem-bers which were also pinned in place. All this was done be-fore any gluing. When the fit was checked and correct everywhere, the ribs were glued in using the small set square to check each one for uprightness and alignment.

The next step required care. Between each pair of ribs the plan called for a piece of balsa with the grain running vertically. These, when glued in, form the shear web. They had to be cut exactly to size, slipped between the ribs and glued. At each end of the centre section of the wing, one of these webs was left out until time to join the outer wings came. Then the upper spar flange was laid in place, making sure it fitted properly and lay flush with the top of every rib before gluing. This method was found easier than the one suggested in the in-structions, which required the spar flange to go in first and the pieces for the web to be cut and slipped in afterwards. Both methods work, however, if done carefully.

The slots for the turbulators were already cut but required a little work with a small file to make them fit correctly.

The outer wings were assembled in the same way as the cen-tre section. In this case, the shear webs of balsa were glued to the rear of the spar flanges, so this was best left until after the upper flange was glued in.

To join the wings together and incorporate the correct dihedral required some careful trimming of the spar ends and fitting plywood braces, already cut exactly to the right shape, in front of and behind the spars. The wing was propped up to the required angle and checked with the set square to ensure there was no misalignment. The glued joint was held, while drying, with an ordinary bulldog clip.

The finished wing is shown here before covering. The leading edge was carefully rounded with the razor plane and sanded smooth, the wing tip blocks were glued on and shaped, then everything carefully sanded with the finest glass paper. Covering, with the iron, is not easy to photograph. Follow the instructions with the roll of film!

Checking the wing for twist. Two lengths of T-section aluminium were used, making sure they were themselves straight first. This was photographed in the garden to get a better light!

The control horns are shown here, mounted on the rudder and elevator, with the control rods cut to length and clipped on. It is best to do this with the servos in place and connected, set to their neutral position, and the control surfaces also neutral so that the rod length is correct.

The control equipment which has to be fitted in the model. From left to right, a 600 mAh nicad battery, a small slide switch, the receiver with aerial and two standard sized servos. The connecting leads are longer than necessary and may be shortened, requiring a little soldering work. None of the items shown here is new – they have all been used in several models over a period of years.

There is not much room to spare! Just behind the nose ballast compartment is the battery, then the receiver, wrapped properly in shock-absorbent foam, and the switch on the fuselage side. Behind this are the two servos, side by side, with their links to the pushrods. In this model the dowels are positioned to take rubber bands running fore and aft. Many other models use crosswise dowels.

A FEW FACTS AND FIGURES

The total weight of the example training glider illustrated in the photographs during construction is 890 grammes (31.4 ounces) completed, ready for flight in all respects. The wing area measured is 0.361 square metres (3.89 sq ft). Dividing the weight by the wing area gives wing loading of 2.45 kg/sq m (8.1 ounces/sq ft) This is typical of this class of model, light and slow in flight. The weight includes:

battery	98g
receiver	34g
2 servos	76g
pushrods and guides	28g
switch	8g
nose ballast	70g
rubber bands	6g
wing	250g
fuselage and tail	320g

chapter ten

BALANCING THE MODEL

THE CENTRE OF GRAVITY

The most important thing when the glider is completed with all the radio gear installed, controls connected and working correctly, warps removed etc., is to make sure the centre of gravity or balance point is in the right place. Probably more new models crash from neglect of this than all other causes.

On a good plan, there will be a clearly marked position for the centre of gravity or CG. If, when otherwise completed, the model does not balance *at or in front of* this point, trimming ballast must be added to the nose. One reason

Balancing the model. With the supports well spaced in the sideways direction and exactly on the main spar, ballast was added in the nose until the model remained in the correct flying attitude. No further movement of the balance point should ever be required. Again the photo was taken in the garden but a calm atmosphere is necessary so the job is best done indoors!

for keeping the tail end of a glider as light as possible is to avoid having to balance it by filling up the front with large amounts of ballast. Placing the battery, servos and receiver as far forward as possible helps to ensure that the CG will come out somewhere near the right place, but this is hardly ever enough.

If the plan does not show it, the CG should be **between one-quarter and one-third** of the **average** distance between the leading edge and trailing edge of the wing. In many cases, this will be **on, or in front of, the main spar**. A rough first check can be made by supporting the model with two fingers, one under each wing. The tips of the fingers should be fairly well apart when this is done, slightly less than half the total span ie about two-fifths of the way out towards the tips (this method works even if the wing has some sweepback, since the effective aerodynamic centre of each wing half is very roughly at the 40–45% spanwise point).

The aim is to get the glider to balance horizontally when the support points are between one-quarter and one-third of the chord measuring from the leading edge. Add nose ballast until the glider takes up a horizontal position when supported in this way. A little nose heaviness is not a bad thing. It makes for *increased safety* if **the CG is a little further forward than the plan shows**.

It is DANGEROUS to have the balance point even slightly too far back.

More accurate measurements can be taken by making a simple wooden support of the kind shown in the diagram (Figs 10.1 and 10.2).

A rearward position of the balance point makes any aircraft, glider or aeroplane, full sized or model, unstable and 'twitchy' in response to the controls. On the other hand, balancing the model well forward reduces the sensitivity and makes for gentle and smooth response. A very experienced pilot may actually like a model which leaps instantly about in response to the merest feather touch but for a beginner this is disastrous. After some successful flying with the CG safely forward, it is worth a little experimenting with balance points to see how much difference it makes to add, or subtract, nose weight. The pilot then can adjust the stability and responsiveness to whatever is preferred. It is incorrect to suppose that moving the CG aft beyond about 35% improves the performance of the model. All it does is to make the elevator more twitchy and the model less stable in flight. If anything it tends to increase drag and hence take a slight edge off the performance.

AVOID THE DIVE TEST

Some modellers advocate a procedure known as the dive test. It is very hard to believe that those who have written about this actually do what they describe. What they recommend is very risky, tends to spoil the performance slightly (if not actually wrecking the glider) and can easily produce a model which in certain circumstances becomes uncontrollable.

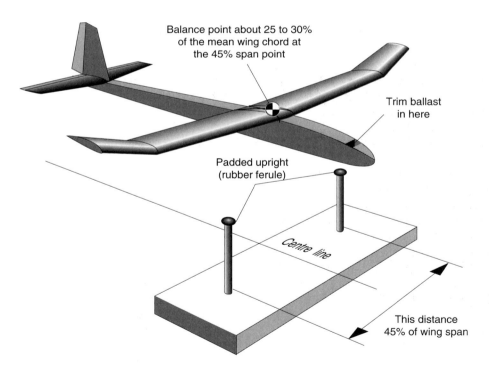

Figure 10.1 *Checking the balance point of the model. Placing supports at about 45% of the span makes an allowance for any wing sweep.*

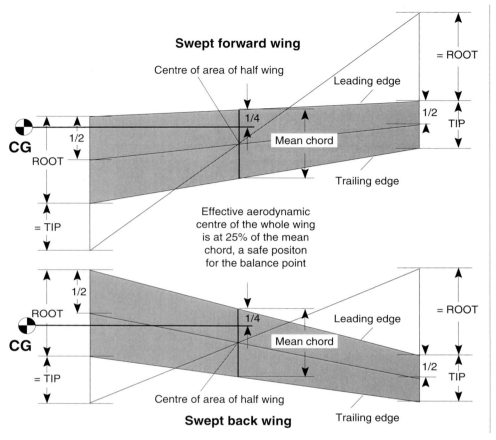

Figure 10.2 *If the wing has a large amount of sweepback or forward, this geometrical construction helps to fix the centre of gravity in a safe position.*

Those who write in favour of the procedure say the model should be dived steeply, say at about 60 degrees, and held in this very steep attitude for some ten or fifteen seconds. Then the elevator stick should be returned to the neutral position. If the model pulls out of the dive rapidly and zooms up, it is claimed, the CG should be moved aft. If, they say, the dive continues unchanged or, at most, the model pulls out very gradually, the CG is in the right place.

A dive at this sort of angle held for such a length of time in practice is more than most model pilots would dare and the model would have to be extremely high beforehand to allow

such a dive for such a length of time. When people try the dive test with their own models, what they actually do usually turns out to be a shallow dive of some thirty degrees held for perhaps three or five seconds.

But there are good reasons for never doing the dive test at all.

A model which does not pull out of a dive when the elevator is neutral (as it should be after releasing the stick), is verging on the unstable. The speed in a steep dive increases very rapidly, the wings begin to twist under the resulting loads, and the margin of stability is further reduced by this. The horizontal tail will also begin to distort. The model is only a hairbreadth away from tucking under. In a **tuck under** the model will go into a steeper dive, there will be even more speed, and the structure distorts so much that the elevator is not powerful enough to bring the model out of the situation. It will dive faster and faster, beyond the vertical into the inverted position and probably hit the ground at very great speed upside down.

If you require a more sensitive elevator, move the CG back very slightly, a few millimetres, try the model in flight and if the elevator is not twitchy enough, try the CG aft a fraction more.

Not all the advice offered by other model fliers is sound. Don't try the dive test!

BALLAST MATERIAL

Plasticine has been used for ballasting models. Bits of scrap iron, small stones, steel balls from bearings, almost anything heavy will do. In an emergency, modellers have been known to place coins in the nose of a glider, which is an unusual sort of investment! Providing the result is a correct centre of gravity, anything is good enough.

The room available in the nose is often small. The best material to use for trim ballast is lead, because it is extremely compact for its mass. Some people use lead shot, which can be bought from ammunition stores and gun dealers. The shot in quantity behaves almost like a liquid and will flow into inaccessible corners inside the nose compartment, filling the available space up. However, although not very dear, shot does cost money and is not ideal. It can spill out as easily as it is poured in. Unless mixed with glue to make a solid lump, a heavy landing can see the ballast thrown out and scattered far and wide.

Scrap dealers sell lead by weight. Find one who has some bits of old roof flashing in thin sheets which can be cut up into tidy squares or rectangles to be glued or even taped into place. Lead can be melted over a gas ring and cast into small blocks or cylinders, if required.

The model completed, ready for its first flight along with another new two-control model, of different design, at the flying field.

Lead may be inserted into the wooden nose block by drilling a hole and pushing some in, with a little glue. If all else fails, the modeller may have to do some reconstruction. To add an extra centimetre to the length of the nose of a glider model, to make a compartment for more trimming ballast, may make all the difference to its flight. A twitchy sailplane can be made very stable in this way, and much more pleasant to fly. Do not attempt to fly if the CG is not right.

LATERAL BALANCE

When completed the two wings should, as far as possible, balance laterally. Set the model upright on a table top and see if one wing always goes down before the other. Usually there will be a difference, especially after repairs. A small imbalance will hardly be detected in flight, but if one wing is noticeably heavy it is best to correct this. Ordinary nails, pushed carefully into the lighter wing tip, can be used. Lead takes less space. Cut a small hole in the lighter wing tip block and insert enough scrap lead to balance. Fix it permanently with a dab of glue in the hole, a wooden plug and a patch of covering plastic over the top. A model which is heavy on one side will fly, but will tend to turn toward the heavy side.

chapter eleven

HOW THE GLIDER FLIES

SUPPORT FROM THE AIR

For a glider or aeroplane to fly, it must keep moving through the air. The airflow caused by its motion must be fast enough to create an **upward reaction force** to **equal the total weight**. If the airspeed is too slow there will not be enough flow and not enough supporting reaction.

It is the airflow over the wing that generates most of the total supporting force. The other parts of the aircraft, tail, fuselage etc., are

In flight! No nasty surprises, the model flew perfectly from a hand launch, then took a full winch launch with ease and on its second flight soared in thermals for half an hour.
The colours chosen were black and orange which show up well against almost any background.

needed to control or **trim** the wing. For the most efficient flight the horizontal tail provides no lift at all, merely being there to keep the model steady.

By trimming the wing at a suitable small angle, called the **angle of attack**, to the flow of air, a **difference of air pressure** arises between the upper and lower surfaces, with less pressure above than below (Fig. 11.1). The angle of attack is controlled by the pilot using the elevator and is also often altered by air gusts and turbulence. Note, this is **not the same as the angle of incidence** which was shown earlier in Fig. 5.3. The angle of attack is the angle at which the air meets the wing. This obviously varies in flight (Fig. 11.2). The angle of incidence is the fixed angle of the wing as it is firmly mounted on the fuselage. Model fliers very often confuse these,

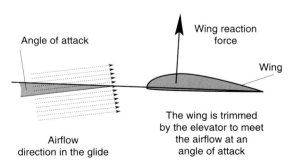

Figure 11.1 *The meaning of angle of attack.*

62

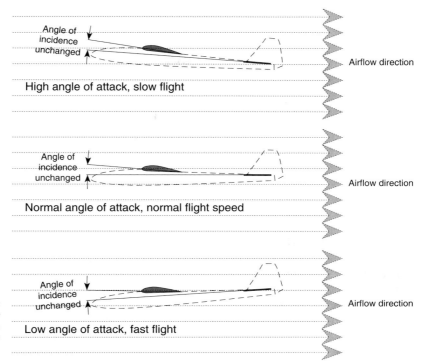

Angle of incidence unchanged

Airflow direction

High angle of attack, slow flight

Angle of incidence unchanged

Airflow direction

Normal angle of attack, normal flight speed

Angle of incidence unchanged

Airflow direction

Low angle of attack, fast flight

Figure 11.2 *Do not confuse angles of attack, which vary during any flight, with the angle of incidence built into the model (compare* **Figure 5.3***).*

so do not be surprised to hear the terms muddled. As well as the angle of attack, the wing section or profile has an important influence on the pressure difference between upper and lower sides of the wing. See Chapter 5 for some remarks about wing sections.

GLIDING

Since a glider has no engine it has to keep itself moving in a manner similar to a bicycle freewheeling down a hill (Fig. 11.3). By tilting the flight path downwards, some of the weight acts to pull glider ahead as well as down. The angle at which the flight path is tilted, is the gliding angle. Note, this is the angle of the flight path, not the angle of the fuselage to the ground.

STALLING

There is a limit to the allowable angle of attack for a wing. If this angle is too large, the airflow will not flow smoothly over the wing but will separate or stall (Fig. 11.4). When the wing stalls the pilot loses control of the glider for a few seconds. The usual behaviour of an aircraft at the stall is a sharp nose down pitch, followed by a dive. If this happens near the ground, a crash or at least a heavy landing is likely.

Stalling when high up is not serious, since control can be regained quickly. To recover from a stall, the elevator must go down first (stick forward) to reduce the wing's angle of attack, and smooth flow returns. The stick then is eased gently back to return to level flight after a brief dive.

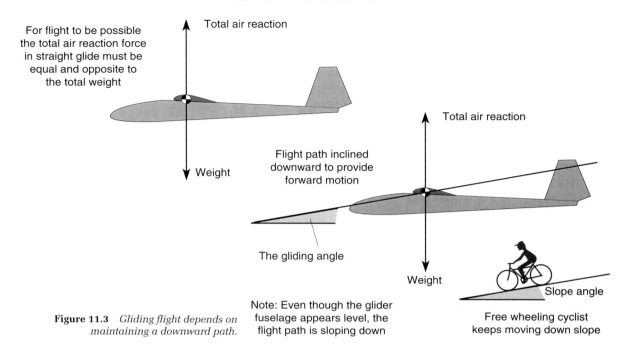

For flight to be possible the total air reaction force in straight glide must be equal and opposite to the total weight

Total air reaction

Weight

Total air reaction

Flight path inclined downward to provide forward motion

The gliding angle

Weight

Slope angle

Figure 11.3 *Gliding flight depends on maintaining a downward path.*

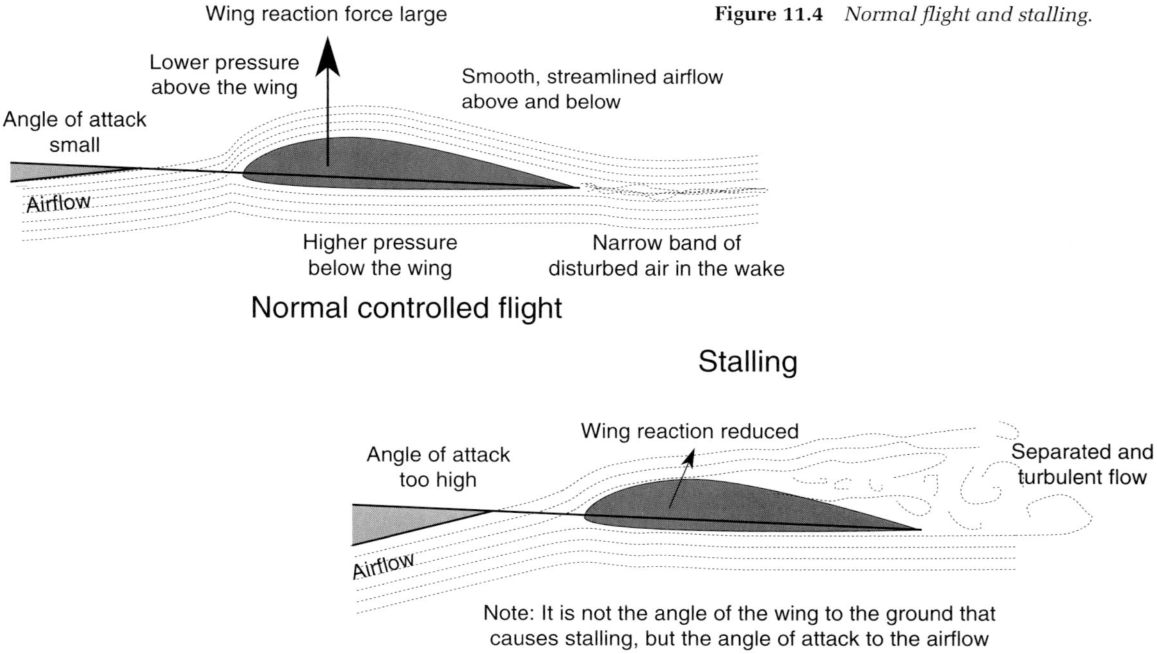

Note: Even though the glider fuselage appears level, the flight path is sloping down

Free wheeling cyclist keeps moving down slope

Wing reaction force large

Lower pressure above the wing

Smooth, streamlined airflow above and below

Figure 11.4 *Normal flight and stalling.*

Angle of attack small

Airflow

Higher pressure below the wing

Narrow band of disturbed air in the wake

Normal controlled flight

Stalling

Wing reaction reduced

Angle of attack too high

Separated and turbulent flow

Airflow

Note: It is not the angle of the wing to the ground that causes stalling, but the angle of attack to the airflow

STALLING SPEED

A freewheeling bicycle on perfectly level ground will gradually slow down and eventually topple over. If the glider tries to follow a perfectly horizontal flight path the airspeed slows down until the air reaction is no longer enough to support the weight. The glider then will cease to support itself, stall and dive until a suitable angle of attack is restored and the air flows smoothly over the wings again.

The airspeed at which this happens is called the **stalling speed**. The stalling speed is the slowest possible airspeed for flight. A glider or aeroplane will stall at a higher speed than this if the angle of attack of the wing is too great.

In a perfect landing, the pilot brings the glider to stalling speed an instant before touching the ground. The run along the ground after landing is then as short as possible.

The stalling speed is the speed of the air over the wing, not the speed of the model over the ground. People very often become quite confused about this. **The airspeed cannot be judged by looking at the ground**. Airspeed against the wind is the same as when flying with the wind, although the ground moves by at different rates below (see remarks later about flying in windy conditions).

THE MINIMUM RATE OF SINK

The rate at which a glider descends through the air is called its rate of sink or **sinking speed** (Fig. 11.5). If the gliding angle is steep, as in a dive, the airspeed rises, but a lot of height is lost. The rate of sink will be very fast. If the glider stalls, it will also come down fast. Somewhere between flying too fast and too slowly is a trim at which the minimum rate of sink is found. In perfectly calm air, trimming at the minimum sinking speed will keep the glider in the air as long as possible in such dead conditions.

A freewheeling bicycle can ride up and over small humps and even low hills, providing some extra speed has been gained down a steep slope first. Similarly a glider can gain enough airspeed, by diving, to enable it to pull up and regain some height, even to do aerobatics, but it will not get back all the height it lost in the dive. Except for such brief temporary gains after diving, a glider always descends relative to the air.

A glider can gain substantial height only by flying in an up current, which is called **soaring**. The glider will go up if the up current is rising faster than the glider's sinking speed. Hence to soar, trimming for the minimum rate of sink is important.

Figure 11.5 *Gliding at different trims and speeds.*

Trimmed for fast glide to cover distance

Trimmed for flight at least rate of sink for soaring

Flying too slowly, danger of stalling

Diving steeply at very high airspeed, losing height very rapidly

Stalled, diving to recover, losing height very rapidly, gaining speed

THE BEST GLIDE ANGLE

At some airspeed faster than that for the least rate of sink, the glider will find its best, or shallowest, angle of glide. This best glide angle or **best glide ratio** is the trim that will give the greatest distance through the air for each metre of height lost, assuming there is no wind, up current or down current. For instance, a best glide ratio of 20 to 1 means that the glider can travel 20 metres through still air for each metre of height. This is **not the same as flying at the least rate of sink**. Flying slower, at minimum sink trim, the glider will not cover so much distance although it will lose less height.

The air is never completely still. If there is wind, or if the glider runs into sinking or rising air, these glide figures will not apply relative to the ground. As with airspeeds, glide angles and rates of sink refer to the air the model is flying in, not to the ground. It is worth giving plenty of thought to this.

LIFT AND DRAG

The best glide ratio is also described as the best Lift/Drag or best L/D ratio. When gliding at a steady airspeed, as mentioned above, the total upward reaction force on the whole glider equals the total weight. The weight always acts directly downwards but it is convenient to think of it as two **force components** (Fig. 11.6). The component which pulls the aircraft along points at a slant directly along the glide slope. The rest of the weight then has to be thought of as acting at right angles to this. The weight itself does not split into two. The division at right angles, or **resolution of the force**, is only a convenient way of thinking.

In the same way, the **total air reaction** can be resolved into two components, one slanting back directly up the glide slope, resisting the pulling force, and the other part at right angles to the glide. These components of the total reaction force are called **drag** and **lift**. In steady, straight flight, the drag is equal to the component of weight acting down the glide path, and the lift is equal to the weight component acting at right angles to the glide path. As before, there is only one force, the air reaction. Lift and drag are convenient ways of dividing this in thought.

With a powered aeroplane in level flight the thrust from the engine equals the drag, the lift then equals the total weight.

If the drag component is large the glider has to keep its airspeed up by flying down a steeply inclined glide path, like a bicycle freewheeling

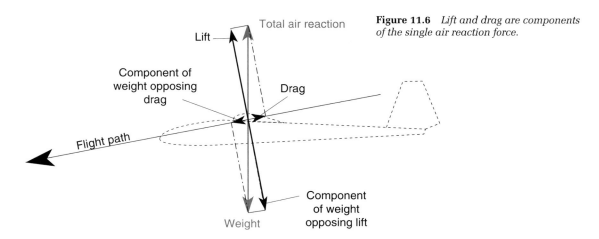

Total air reaction

Lift

Component of weight opposing drag

Drag

Flight path

Weight

Component of weight opposing lift

Figure 11.6 *Lift and drag are components of the single air reaction force.*

downhill with the brakes partly on. A glider with **large drag** will have a **poor glide**. The airbrakes on a sailplane give the pilot a means of increasing drag and so spoiling the glide, which is very useful for landing.

If the glider has to cover a large distance, as it often will, if it has low drag it will not require a steep dive to gain speed but will accelerate quickly with quite a shallow glide angle. It will have a good glide ratio at high speed. This is called **penetration**. Improving the performance of a glider at both high and low airspeeds means reducing drag.

TYPES OF WING DRAG

Most of the drag of a glider comes from the wing. Since the wing must move through the air to provide lift, wing drag is inescapable, but it can be reduced by careful design. Wing drag is of two kinds, vortex drag (often called induced drag) and profile drag.

VORTEX DRAG

Near the wing tips, air tends to spill from the underside round to the upper side where the pressure is lower (Fig. 11.7). This creates whirling wing tip vortices and much energy is lost. To reduce vortex drag the wing may be made very long and narrow with a large span and small chord. This high aspect ratio design is seen on all high performance sailplanes, model and full sized. Tapering the wing a little in plan, making the tips narrower than the root, also helps. The shape of the extreme tips has some influence, though not very great. Vertical **winglets** on some aircraft are intended to reduce the tip vortex and so save drag.

Reducing vortex drag is extremely important for soaring at minimum sinking speed trim. It does not matter so much at higher airspeeds.

PROFILE DRAG

The drag of the wing profile or aerofoil section is important, especially for fast flying. A thin wing section with small camber will create less drag when flying fast than a thick one, but it will cause an increase in drag and may stall when flying slowly for soaring (Fig. 11.8). The thickness of the profile is also very important when designing the wing structure. To find space inside a thin wing for strong spars is very difficult. To make thin wings strong they tend to

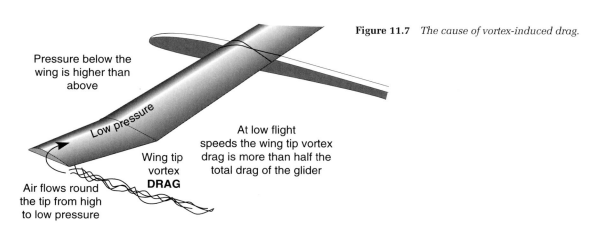

Figure 11.7 *The cause of vortex-induced drag.*

Pressure below the wing is higher than above

Low pressure

Wing tip vortex **DRAG**

At low flight speeds the wing tip vortex drag is more than half the total drag of the glider

Air flows round the tip from high to low pressure

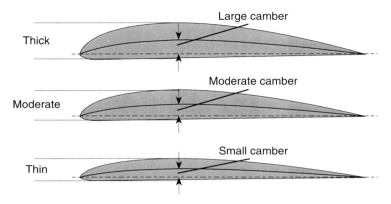

Figure 11.8 *Wing profiles. Three aerofoil sections, all flat bottomed for easy construction but with very different camber and thickness, so having very different flying characteristics.*

become heavy. Expensive materials may have to be used in their construction to avoid this. A thick wing can be stronger and lighter but because it has high drag at high speeds the glider may not perform so well when required to fly fast. A wing with a lot of camber will give low drag at low speeds and high drag when flying fast. The designer has to compromise in all these things to achieve a good result.

PARASITIC DRAG

Drag also comes from the tail, the fuselage, and every other part of a glider that is exposed to the airflow, including projecting control horns, gaps and awkward corners which the air is forced to flow through. Such drag is called parasitic drag. Parasitic drag can be reduced by careful design and attention to detail, such as streamlining the fuselage, but the gains are much less than are obtained by reducing wing drag.

chapter twelve

HOW THE GLIDER CONTROLS WORK

THE ELEVATOR

Part of the tail of every ordinary model glider is a movable surface called the elevator. When the model is flying, if the trailing or rear edge of the elevator goes down, the airflow over the surface responds by raising the tail and this tilts the nose down. So, pushing the **transmitter stick forward** applies **down elevator** and pitches the model **nose-down**, decreasing the angle of attack of the wing (Fig. 12.1). The airspeed rises because the glide is steeper. A small down elevator movement will cause a slight nose-down pitch and a small gain of speed.

Putting the elevator fully down will quickly force the model into a steep dive. It will gain airspeed fast and lose height very quickly. In an extreme case, full down elevator can push the

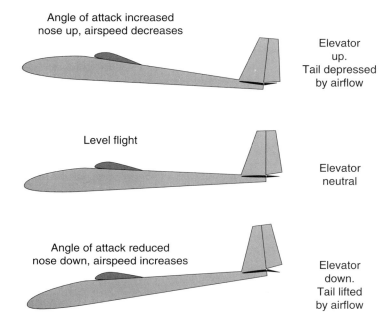

Angle of attack increased
nose up, airspeed decreases

Elevator
up.
Tail depressed
by airflow

Level flight

Elevator
neutral

Angle of attack reduced
nose down, airspeed increases

Elevator
down.
Tail lifted
by airflow

Figure 12.1 *Controls. The action of the elevator is to raise and lower the nose so causing the angle of attack to change and hence varying the airspeed.*

model beyond the vertical, in what is known as a **bunt**, into the upside-down position. This is sometimes done deliberately in aerobatics.

Moving the **elevator up** will cause the airflow to depress the tail and the nose of the glider will rise, **increasing the angle of attack**. Up elevator causes nose-up pitch and a reduction in airspeed. Too much reduction of airspeed and a high angle of attack will stall the wing.

A glider cannot be made to climb continuously by using up elevator. When the elevator is raised gently, the model may gain a little height for a few seconds but will soon settle into a slow glide, perhaps with its nose tilted up a little but nevertheless descending through the air with the wing at a high angle of attack, almost stalling.

Full up elevator will cause a very sharp nose-up pitch. If this is done during a glide at normal airspeed, the model will stall and dive at once. When flying fast, up elevator movement may still bring the wing to the stalling angle even though the airspeed is high. Such a **high speed stall** may cause the glider to fall out of a steep turn, or, in aerobatics, may be used to make a 'flick' roll.

Stalling near the ground is probably the main cause of damage to a beginner's first model glider. Naturally enough, the temptation is to slow the descent to make the final landing as gentle as possible, so the elevator stick creeps back and an unwanted stall is brought on. Airspeed must be maintained until the last possible moment before touchdown. It is better to land a little too fast and skid a long way or skip slightly into the air again, than to stall a couple of metres up and drop heavily, nose down into the ground.

THE RUDDER

The primary result of moving the **rudder** is to **yaw** the model (Fig. 12.2). Moving the transmitter stick to the right causes the rudder to move

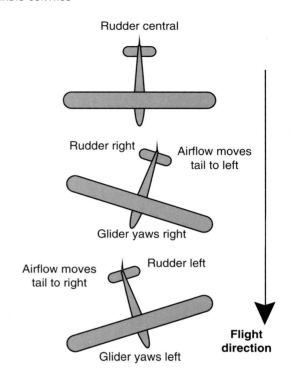

Figure 12.2 *The primary effect of the rudder. Right rudder, right yaw: left rudder, left yaw.*

to the right or starboard side of the glider. The airflow reacts by moving the tail to the left and hence, yawing the whole model to the right. Right stick, right rudder, right yaw. Conversely, left rudder gives left yaw.

TURNING

Unlike a boat, an aircraft does not necessarily follow its nose. Yawing with the rudder does not immediately give a turn. To obtain a turn, a force is needed to move the whole glider. **The only part of the aircraft that is capable of producing such a force efficiently is the wing.** The lift normally acts generally upwards but if the wing can be tilted, or banked, some of the lift is directed sideways and a turn results. It is only

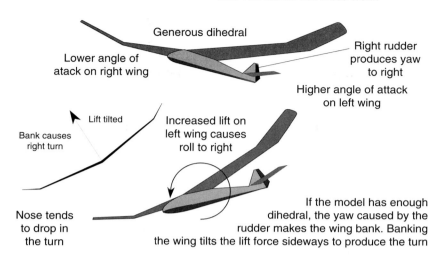

Generous dihedral

Lower angle of
atack on right wing

Right rudder
produces yaw
to right

Higher angle of attack
on left wing

Lift tilted

Bank causes
right turn

Increased lift on
left wing causes
roll to right

Nose tends
to drop in
the turn

If the model has enough
dihedral, the yaw caused by the
rudder makes the wing bank. Banking
the wing tilts the lift force sideways to produce the turn

Figure 12.3 *How the rudder causes a model with dihedral to turn. Note: if the wing does not bank, no turn results.*

when the wing is banked that the model will turn properly. **No bank, no turn!**

On the first model glider the rudder is also used for turning because it has a secondary effect (Fig. 12.3). Turning is achieved by building the wing with pronounced dihedral or polyhedral so that when it is yawed it immediately banks.

With enough dihedral, as soon as the rudder causes a yaw, say to the right, the wing on the left-hand side of the glider finds itself meeting the air at a higher angle of attack and the lift on that side increases. On the other side, the angle of attack is reduced and the lift falls. The difference in the lift on the two wings banks the entire model over and the inclined lift force turns the glider. Yawing is followed by a banking of the wing.

It is always wrong to try to turn without banking. This explains one of the most obvious features of the two-control type of model. The rudder–elevator controlled sailplane relies on the rudder to yaw the model, the dihedral then banks it over, and the wing lift produces the turn. If the model does not respond well to the rudder, increasing the dihedral is likely to improve it. A model with no dihedral will not turn effectively unless it has ailerons to bank the wing.

ELEVATOR CO-ORDINATION IN THE TURN

For steady flight, the total upward air reaction force must always support the weight. When the wing is banked over to turn the glider, some of the normal upward support force is being diverted to the side. The loss in upward support has to be made up or the glider will lose height. The wing has to be made to operate at a higher angle of attack because it has to provide both the turning force and also support the weight.

The elevator controls the angle of attack of the wing. As the glider **banks**, the **elevator** at the same time should move **up slightly** (Fig. 12.4). When done correctly, an efficient banked turn results. However, increasing the angle of attack of the wing always takes it nearer to the stalling angle. When flying slowly, doing a turn may cause an unwanted stall. To avoid this, the airspeed should always be a little higher when turning.

AILERONS

The purpose of ailerons is to bank the wing directly without having to rely on rudder yaw and dihedral to force the bank (Fig. 12.5). As a

71

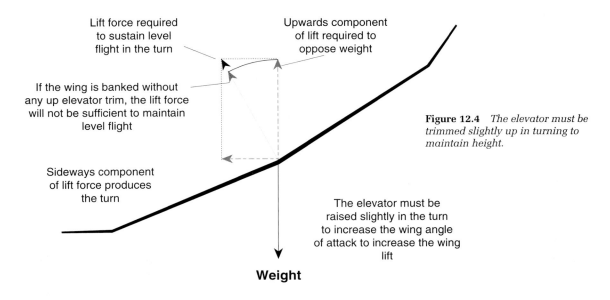

Lift force required
to sustain level
flight in the turn

Upwards component
of lift required to
oppose weight

If the wing is banked without
any up elevator trim, the lift force
will not be sufficient to maintain
level flight

Figure 12.4 *The elevator must be trimmed slightly up in turning to maintain height.*

Sideways component
of lift force produces
the turn

The elevator must be
raised slightly in the turn
to increase the wing angle
of attack to increase the wing
lift

Weight

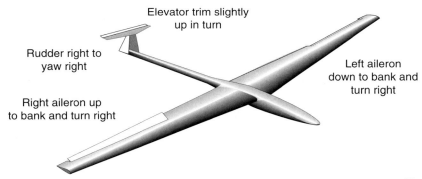

Elevator trim slightly
up in turn

Rudder right to
yaw right

Left aileron
down to bank and
turn right

Right aileron up
to bank and turn right

Ailerons are the primary control for banking and turning

Figure 12.5 *Ailerons.*

primary turning control, the ailerons are more effective. A model glider which has ailerons will need very little dihedral or none at all.

The ailerons are hinged to the trailing edge of the wings and as **one moves up the other goes down**. The air reaction is then to drive the wing down on the side which has aileron up, and up on the side with aileron down. The glider turns to the side of the up aileron. Banking the model still requires co-ordinated elevator control. In a turn the wing angle of attack has to increase so the elevator has to be trimmed up.

Right stick on the transmitter, **right aileron up**, **right-handed bank**, **right-handed turn** and of course, left stick, left aileron up, left turn.

RUDDER CO-ORDINATION

The down aileron creates more lift on that side but also more vortex-induced drag on the upgoing wing (the tip vortex becomes stronger). This tends to pull the wing back and yaw the glider in the wrong direction for the turn. To overcome this adverse aileron drag, the rudder is used to counteract it. To enter a right turn smoothly with ailerons requires **right aileron and right rudder together**. On many gliders the rudder and the ailerons are linked mechanically or by electronic coupling of controls in the transmitter.

AIRBRAKES AND SPOILERS

Spoilers are hinged plates which normally lie flat, flush with the upper surface of the wing. They open when required to stand up against the airflow. Airbrakes do the same job but rise up vertically through slots (Fig. 12.6).

Airbrakes and spoilers, when open, create extra drag, so spoiling the glide, making it steeper. This is a great help when judging a landing. Without brakes or spoilers, as the glider gets near to the ground it tends to float for a long distance before touching down. If the model approaching to land looks like going too far, the brakes, if any, can be opened. Brakes are also very useful if the sailplane is high and the pilot needs to bring it down quickly. If dived without brakes, it will gain too much airspeed, which may cause serious damage. With brakes open the model can be brought down steeply without danger.

Opening either brakes or spoilers often causes the glider to pitch nose-down. The pilot has to be prepared for this and meet the change with prompt elevator control. This can be achieved automatically with some of the more expensive radios.

Many beginners hesitate to fit spoilers or brakes to their models and it is true that there is a good deal of extra complication in constructing them and getting them to work correctly. It is necessary to make sure the spoilers do close fully when required, and lock shut. In flight spoilers can sometimes be sucked slightly open, this being caused by the reduced air pressure on the upper side of the wing. They also have to open equally on the two wings, when called on.

An extra servo will also be needed, maybe two. If the brakes are to be operated by one servo and this is mounted in the fuselage, some sort of mechanical linkages, wires, strings or drive rods, will be required and these will have to come apart when the wing is removed. This is not easy to arrange. Quite often the spoilers either do not shut properly in flight, or refuse to come open equally, because the linkage at the wing root is not completely secure. Many model builders prefer to use two very small servos (which cost more than the standard sizes), mounted close to the brakes, one in each wing with extended electrical leads. Then the only connection required at the wing root is a miniature electrical plug which 'floats', allowing flexibility. This gives reliable operation even if the wing shifts slightly.

If the wing is in one piece from tip to tip, the brake or spoiler servo can be fixed in the wing

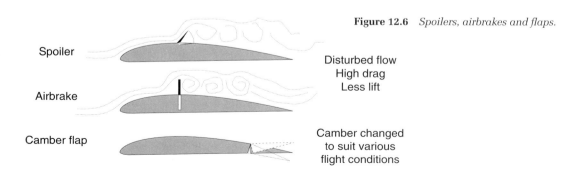

Figure 12.6 *Spoilers, airbrakes and flaps.*

Spoiler

Airbrake

Camber flap

Disturbed flow
High drag
Less lift

Camber changed
to suit various
flight conditions

root to drive pushrods in both directions. This is very safe but somewhat inconvenient for transporting the model.

If the extra work can be done, it is nevertheless well worth the effort to fit brakes or spoilers. The touchdown point can be judged more accurately when landing, and the sailplane will not be so easily lost upwards in strong up currents. It is, of course, necessary to learn how to use these controls, allowing for trim changes when they are opened or shut, but this may be postponed until confidence has been gained in flying without them.

FLAPS

The first model should not have flaps but these are used on advanced sailplanes to change the wing section to suit different conditions. Drooping the flaps increases the wing camber, which decreases drag at slow airspeeds, so reducing the minimum rate of sink, which is important for soaring. Raising the flaps reduces the wing camber and enables the sailplane to fly fast with low drag, which is necessary for flying without too much loss of height from one thermal to another, or in certain types of competitions and races.

chapter thirteen

LEARNING TO FLY

A book cannot teach anyone to fly. It has to be learned by getting a glider into the air and practising. As mentioned earlier, although people have taught themselves, frustrations, broken models and disappointments are certain. Avoid most of this by getting an instructor for the early stages. But even with help, be prepared for some difficulties at first.

The best way to find an instructor is through a model flying club, and/or on a personal basis. Make a definite appointment with the instructor for a particular day and time, rather than just arriving at a flying ground and hoping to find someone. No-one is paid to teach model flying so everything is on a friendly basis, but instructors like to fly their own models sometimes and will not always be anxious to teach.

With instruction the process of learning is quite quick and the 'solo' pilot can go on with confidence. That is not to say there will never be setbacks. Everyone makes mistakes and models have to be repaired from time to time.

STABILITY

Long before there was any radio control, model sailplanes flew perfectly well and often made good soaring flights, with no means whatever of controlling them after launching. They were designed for stability. If anything happened in the air to upset them, they were capable of straightening themselves out and continuing quite safely. Such **free-flight** models are still flown.

A model glider **will fly by itself** if it has the centre of gravity in the right place, is trimmed properly, and launched with all the controls held in their neutral position. The disadvantage is that the model may wander away and be lost, or hit an obstruction on landing. All the same, remember that the model would fly very nicely with all controls neutral if it were simply left alone! Beginners almost always do too much, rather than too little, with the controls.

PREPARING FOR FLIGHT

Get into good habits from the very beginning. Make a check list of everything that needs to be done before flight. Some things should be attended to at home the night before, like putting the batteries on charge, or ensuring that any necessary repair or maintenance work has been done. Inspect the glider for damage. Go over the structure in an orderly way, from tip to tip on the wing, looking for unnoticed dents, cracks, punctures. On the fuselage start at the nose and work back to the tail. Make sure all hinges are secure but free to move as they are required to do. Give special attention to pushrods, control horns, servo mountings. If repairs are needed, do not attempt to fly until they have been done.

Go over the launching equipment, if any, to ensure it is serviceable. Go through the list while loading the car or filling the model box, making sure that nothing vital is left behind. An astonishing number of pilots turn up at the flying field without something vital, such as the transmitter, or rubber bands to hold the wing on, or even the wing itself! Pack very carefully. Models are often damaged in transit.

On arrival at the flying site, assemble the glider. Check that the transmitter frequency is clear. When it is so, take the appropriate frequency peg or put your tag on the board, switch on transmitter and receiver and ensure that the radio is operating correctly. Are all controls working the right way round, with correct amounts of movement? Do a ground check of range, with help from your instructor or anyone who knows what is required.

If anything is wrong, put it right before attempting to fly. On your first few occasions out with a new model, the instructor will probably want to check everything again but it will have done no harm for you to go through the procedure yourself.

When this pre-flight routine has become automatic, beware! All too often human beings become so accustomed to going through drills that they fail to think about the purpose of the

drill, merely going through the motions. Make every inspection a real inspection. It is an excellent practice to have a written check list, like that offered on page 99, and physically check off each item. Add to the check list anything special that is required for your particular situation.

THE FIRST FLIGHT

The first flight of a new model is always a slightly anxious time, even for an expert. The glider may be hand launched to do a simple test glide (Fig. 13.1). This is intended only to give the model enough airspeed to fly for a short distance. The glider is held in its normal flying attitude, slightly nose-down. The launcher may run forward a few steps into the wind to get up speed and give the model an extra push but there is no great effort involved and no attempt to get the glider up high. The person launching can feel when the air reaction is enough to carry the weight, and only a little more speed than this is required for a smooth launch. All being well, the glider floats for 50 metres or so, under the instructor's full control, and lands smoothly.

There is some argument about the wisdom of hand-launched test glides, because if the trim turns out to be wrong there is little time to make adjustments. A sharp dive immediately after launching indicates too much elevator down trim. This is very difficult even for an expert to catch in time and the model may land heavily, nose-down and fast. The opposite, too much up

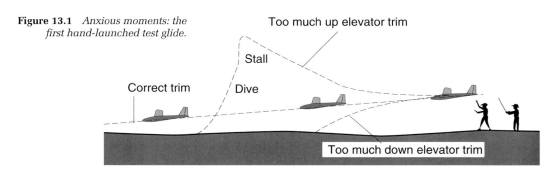

Figure 13.1 *Anxious moments: the first hand-launched test glide.*

Too much up elevator trim

Stall

Correct trim

Dive

Too much down elevator trim

trim, causes a climb and stall, with the usual nose-down pitch and dive which, again, may be too quick for corrective action. A sudden swerve to left or right can cause a cart wheeling **ground loop**. These things should not happen if the model was built accurately to the plan, and the initial checking and balancing done, but they do sometimes occur.

HILL SOARING HAND LAUNCH

A hand launch from a hill top immediately into an up-slope wind is safer (Fig. 13.2). If the trim is not right the extra space immediately ahead gives the test pilot more room to recover before hitting anything. Height is soon gained in the slope up current and may be used to give the trims a thorough check. It is also easier for a beginner to learn to fly by hill soaring, since each flight lasts longer than from a bungee or towline launch.

TOWLINE TEST FLIGHT

At a flat site the instructor may decide to take the model up at once on a bungee, hand tow or winch line. If the model is slightly out of trim an experienced pilot should still be able to get it up safely and the trimming controls on the transmitter can be adjusted after dropping the line.

Some alterations will almost always be needed after the first few test flights. Adding lead to the nose ballast and changing the length of the elevator pushrod (by screwing a link in or out), are likely requirements.

THE FIRST INSTRUCTIONAL FLIGHT

After the elementary tests, the instructor will probably take the model into the air again, if the weather is suitable, and let the beginner feel the control movements as the instructor makes them. (There are special transmitters equipped for training with a 'buddy box' containing a duplicate set of controls plugged in. These outfits are rather costly, however, and not often available.) Alternatively, the pupil may take the transmitter in hand but the instructor will be poised to take it back if necessary.

THE INSTRUCTOR

The trainee pilot is usually very nervous. It is important for the instructor to anticipate trouble

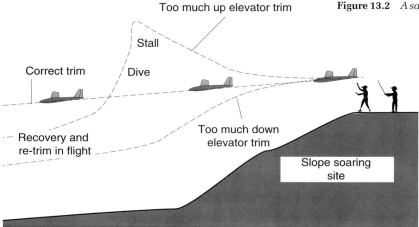

Figure 13.2 *A safer procedure for the first test flight.*

Too much up elevator trim

Stall

Correct trim

Dive

Recovery and re-trim in flight

Too much down elevator trim

Slope soaring site

and take over control before it gets too serious, but the student pilot will learn best if the small mistakes are corrected by the person who makes them. As far as possible, the instructor should quietly tell the student what is wrong, advise a gentle corrective action in good time, and let the student attempt it, taking over only if things are really getting out of control.

Nothing is likely to make the beginner more anxious and more prone to over control, than an instructor who suddenly starts shouting, or makes a sudden last second grab for the transmitter without warning, and maybe too late. If things begin to go wrong the pupil may start all kinds of extraordinary motions in desperation or, very commonly, 'freeze' altogether, gazing in horror as the glider goes into a steep, spiralling dive, or swoops up and down in a series of stalls and dives. An instructor who, at such a time, also starts raving in an excited fashion, will complete the novice's demoralisation. The instructor should recognise the difficulty before it arises if possible, and intervene with a calm word or two at first, giving the student time to hear, understand, and do something, rather than uttering sudden commands, seizing the transmitter, or putting on a demonstration of hysteria.

Both pupil and instructor should be prepared to take rests now and then. It is best not to attempt too much in the first hour. Most beginners feel quite tired after three or four instructional flights. Take a rest and watch other people flying. Listen to the talk and learn from it (but don't believe absolutely everything you hear!).

At first, as when learning to drive a car, it seems as if everything has to be learned at once. The instructor will try to teach one thing at a time but this is not entirely possible. The accompanying list of exercises, which may be done at a slope site or, after a good high launch over flat ground, will give the student pilot something to aim at. The instructor may like to check each item off as it is mastered, which boosts the pupil's confidence. Model fliers do not usually keep log books, in the way pilots of full-sized sailplanes do, for instructors to check through and write comments in, but this is a good idea, especially if more than one instructor is involved in the teaching. In particular, if a pilot goes to a flat site after hill soaring or vice versa, or joins a new club, a log book helps to establish the type of help that may be needed.

PROGRESSIVE EXERCISES

Learning to fly is progressive, beginning with simple exercises and going on to more difficult ones. The first exercise, beginning when the model is in a steady, straight glide, is to let it continue straight and level (though gliding down) without any control action. Perhaps the instructor should let this continue for some time, to impress the trainee with the safe, stable characteristics of the model. Learning when to do nothing is one of the first lessons!

Because of gusts in the air or some slight, uncorrected bias in the model, the glider will not continue for ever flying straight, but will begin to turn one way or the other. The pupil should correct this and bring the model back to straight flight.

A little pressure on the rudder control stick in the appropriate sense is needed. The pilot moves the stick. There is a delay: nothing seems to happen (Fig. 13.3). Naturally enough the novice fears the worst and tends to push the stick more and suddenly it seems the glider has canted violently over, is hurtling earthwards and the instructor has to take over!

The model does not respond to controls instantly. It cannot do so. The servo needs a moment to move, the control surface shifts, the airflow changes, and the glider only then begins to react.

The **most common error is to over-control**. The delayed response of the model seems to require some forceful action by the pilot, so the control is moved more sharply than necessary.

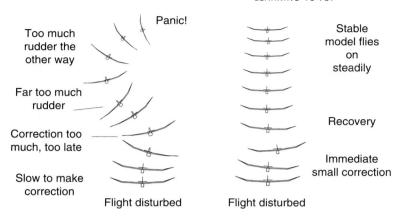

Figure 13.3 *Over-controlling: a common fault with beginners.*

This, when it takes effect, produces a bigger reaction by the model than is required. The pilot anxiously tries to correct this with another vigorous control action the other way, so the model swings violently back and things get worse progressively, with the pilot pump-handling the control stick until the glider is gyrating all over the sky.

Make a small control movement, wait, watch the model carefully. Don't fiddle with the controls if it is not necessary. Remember the model will fly by itself if the controls are neutral. Let it settle down.

MAKING A DELIBERATE TURN

From learning how to keep straight, the next step comes quite naturally: getting the model to turn to right and left as the pilot commands.

Begin with gentle turns, which demand only small rudder control pressures. Think of this as **persuading** the model to bank, rather than forcing it. The wing will turn the model when the bank has been established, so, as always, give time for the reaction, watch, and adjust. Remember that it is the banked wing, not the rudder, which causes the glider to turn.

SOME EXERCISES FOR THE BEGINNER

1 STRAIGHT FLIGHT, correcting any deviations, keeping airspeed steady
2 PERFORMING A TURN TO RIGHT OR LEFT, straighten out on a chosen heading, control airspeed throughout
3 RECOVER FROM A STALL, restoring straight and level flight
4 FLY AN 'S' TURN, emerging straight and level on the previous heading at the same airspeed
5 FLY A COMPLETE CIRCLE, keeping airspeed and bank angle steady
6 FLY THREE CONSECUTIVE CIRCLES at constant bank and steady airspeed
7 CONSECUTIVE CIRCLES IN ONE DIRECTION (bank and speed steady)
8 TURNS AT DIFFERENT ANGLES OF BANK
9 FLIGHT TO A PATTERN SPECIFIED BEFORE TAKE OFF
10 FLY A SQUARE APPROACH (instructor does landing)
11 CARRY OUT TOWLINE LAUNCH (instructor helping)
12 FLY COMPLETE CIRCUIT, LAUNCH, APPROACH AND LANDING
13 ATTEMPT LAUNCH, CIRCUIT AND LANDING INDEPENDENTLY
14 ATTEMPT SOARING INDEPENDENTLY

Even a slight bank will cause the glider's nose to go down a little (see Chapter 12 *How the glider controls work* for an explanation of this). A small **elevator** up action should be **co-ordinated** as the bank comes on. Move the controls gently, wait, watch and make small adjustments. In this way, a feel for controlling the aircraft will develop until the movements are automatic and made more boldly.

It is not always easy to judge the attitude of the glider from the ground. This comes with practice. Watch the angle made by the fuselage to the horizontal, and keep this as constant as possible with the elevator. Remember that the airspeed rises if the nose goes down, and speed falls if the nose is allowed to rise. If the model is directly overhead it is impossible to judge the angle, so, at first, avoid flying overhead. If you become unsure of the attitude and speed at any time, remember stability. If the controls are centralised, the glider will try to settle to a normal flying attitude of its own accord.

CENTRALISE THE RUDDER

The rudder is there to start the turn by yawing and so banking the wing. It is not needed to keep the turn going.

Once the bank has been established and the model begins to turn, the rudder should be returned to central because, if it is kept on, it will yaw the model further than required and the bank will get steeper (Fig. 13.4). So long as the wing is banked and the elevator slightly up a stable glider will tend to remain turning even if the rudder is centralised.

If the rudder is kept on when the model is banked, the yaw so brought about not only increases the bank but also forces the nose of the glider down. In the extreme case, if the bank is vertical or nearly so, the rudder's yawing action becomes equivalent to the elevator. The airspeed increases and a spiral dive results.

ANTICIPATION

When it is time to straighten out and return to level flight, the rudder is used to get the wing level again. The model will not immediately snap back to straight flight. The signal goes, the servo moves, the rudder is deflected against the turn. The model yaws away from the turn and the dihedral acts to bring the wings level. It always takes a little time. As soon as the bank is off, the turn stops. Centralise the controls again a little before the bank is all gone.

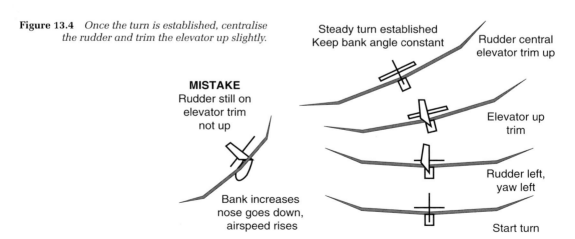

Figure 13.4 *Once the turn is established, centralise the rudder and trim the elevator up slightly.*

Steady turn established
Keep bank angle constant

Rudder central
elevator trim up

Elevator up
trim

Rudder left,
yaw left

Start turn

MISTAKE
Rudder still on
elevator trim
not up

Bank increases
nose goes down,
airspeed rises

When coming out of a turn, the glider will have too much angle of attack for level flight, because in the turn the elevator was up slightly. As the wings come level this will cause it to surge upwards a little. The up elevator needed to stay in the turn should come off as the wings come level and a whisper of down elevator may be needed to bring the glider to its slightly nose-down, straight glide position. Elevators are more sensitive than rudders, so be gentle.

COPING WITH THE STALL

At some stage early in the learning process, the glider will stall (Fig. 13.5). This is only serious if it happens close to the ground. The stall may be caused by a sudden gust of wind or turbulence in the air, but more likely it will be the pilot's action, or inaction, that brings this about. An elevator correction is not given, or given too late. The model raises its nose, climbs slightly, and the stall-pitch-dive comes. By this time the pilot may have recognised that something is not quite right and thinks of moving the elevator stick forward to catch the stall before it happens,

a moment too late, because the glider has already, of its own accord, pitched nose-down. The pilot's action tips the glider even more nose-down and it dives rather steeply. The novice pulls the stick back sharply to correct this, the model surges up and another, more violent stall follows. Now the pilot is pumping the stick back and forth, always a little too late, and the whole process goes wrong.

Watch all the time and anticipate. As the model's nose **starts** to rise, give a little down elevator to keep the nose in the regular gliding position (Fig. 13.6). Preventing the stall is a matter of keeping the wing's angle of attack within limits, which requires judging the attitude relative to the air.

If the glider stalls anyway, don't worry (Fig. 13.7). Its natural stability will help the recovery. Stick forward a little to reduce the angle of attack, let it pick up speed and then ease out of the dive with up elevator. As it approaches level again check the upward surge with a little forward motion of the stick. Timing comes with practice.

When this has become easier, try some deliberate stalls. With plenty of height in hand, flying

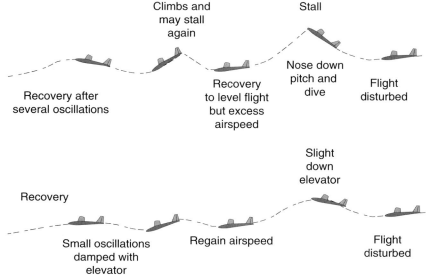

Climbs and may stall again

Stall

Nose down pitch and dive

Flight disturbed

Recovery to level flight but excess airspeed

Recovery after several oscillations

Figure 13.5 *A stable aircraft will always attempt to return to its trimmed flight attitude without any action by the pilot, but will tend to oscillate for some time.*

Slight down elevator

Recovery

Small oscillations damped with elevator

Regain airspeed

Flight disturbed

Figure 13.6 *If the pilot recognises the approach of a stall, a small down elevator action will restore the attitude and further oscillations will be easily damped.*

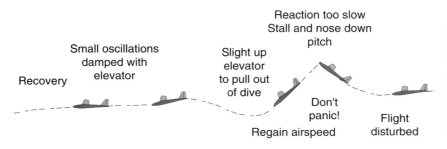

Recovery — Small oscillations damped with elevator — Slight up elevator to pull out of dive — Reaction too slow Stall and nose down pitch — Don't panic! — Regain airspeed — Flight disturbed

Figure 13.7 *If the pilot is a little slow to recognise the disturbance the model may stall unexpectedly. Keep the nose down briefly to regain airspeed, then pull gently out of the dive and recover with slight elevator movements to damp out oscillations.*

straight and level, pull the elevator smoothly to its fully up position. The glider will stall and pitch forward. Stick neutral and watch. The model will go into its stalled dive, gain speed and pull itself out of the dive without any action by the pilot. Quite a lot of height will be lost but then the nose will rise and the model will rotate upwards again and another stall comes. This is what a stable glider does, trying to correct itself, but the first correction goes too far, rather like a pendulum that swings back and forth several times before finally settling. The glider goes through a series of diving and climbing and stalling motions. It will do quite a few of these before the natural stability smooths the flight out.

Don't let the up and down motions go on so long that the height is all used up before level flight returns. Just before a stall, use down elevator to bring the nose to the proper attitude. Practise this exercise repeatedly until the timing is right every time, so that you can prevent a stall developing, or, if the model has stalled, bring it back to level again without hesitation. The idea is to become familiar with stalling, but not contemptuous!

INCIPIENT SPIN

Try stalling deliberately in a turn, by using too much up elevator. Notice that one wing goes down sharply as the model stalls. This wing dropping or tip stalling is very common. It is caused by one wing stalling more severely than

the other, which is almost impossible to avoid if the model stalls while turning. The wing which is further into the stall creates extra drag and so forces the whole model to twirl round. This is the beginning of a spin. Use down elevator to unstall the wing, straighten up with the rudder and pull out of the dive when airspeed has recovered.

A fully aerobatic model will go into a full spin from such a wing-dropping stall. This is done deliberately in aerobatics, but a beginner's model will probably refuse to spin fully. It will, nonetheless, stall if the airspeed is too slow in the turn, roll over sharply and dive – an incipient spin. Do not use too much up elevator in the turn and don't stall when turning near the ground. Spinning deliberately can be left until the pilot has flown a few different models and is looking for some excitement.

The recovery from a spin depends always on unstalling the wing. If the model is truly spinning, centralise all the controls, use rudder to stop or reduce the rotation, and down elevator to reduce the wing's angle of attack. When airspeed has recovered, pull out of the dive gently. Do not pull the stick back sharply because this can cause another stall immediately, with another spin following.

SPIRAL DIVE

A spiral dive is not a spin and does not even look the same. In a true spin the model is stalled and rotates around its own axis, descending rapidly but not at a high airspeed. In a spiral dive it flies round a diving circle, not stalled and picking up speed rapidly. This can be dangerous if the speed is allowed to get too high. Remember that a turn is caused by bank combined with up elevator.

Pulling more up elevator while the wing is still banked, will tighten the turn. Such a fast turning dive can pull the wings off. To recover from a spiral dive, centralise the elevator first and get the wings level with a little rudder against the turn. When the model is straight with elevators still neutral, stability will start to bring the nose up again. Gently help it out of the dive with very careful up elevator.

FLYING AWAY AND FLYING BACK

When the glider is flying away from the pilot the action of the controls seems quite natural. A right pressure on the rudder stick causes a right-hand bank and the glider turns to the pilot's right, and vice versa, left stick, left bank, motion to the left.

If the glider is flying directly towards the pilot, this seems to be the other way round (Fig. 13.8). A right-hand stick movement causes the starboard or right-hand wing of the glider to go down and the glider turns accordingly. But because it is heading towards the pilot, the resulting motion is to the pilot's left side.

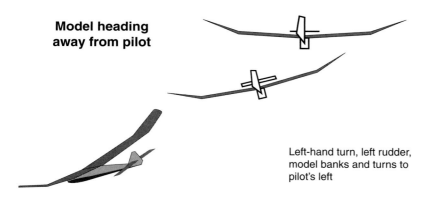

Model heading away from pilot

Figure 13.8 *Flying away and flying back.*

Left-hand turn, left rudder, model banks and turns to pilot's left

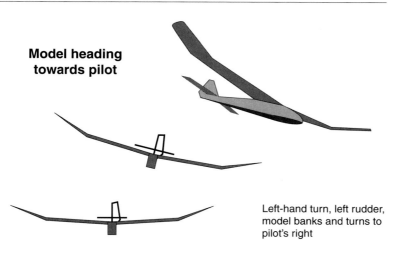

Model heading towards pilot

Left-hand turn, left rudder, model banks and turns to pilot's right

A good many people find this difficult to adjust to and tend to make the wrong control movements when the glider is heading homewards. Some of those finding most difficulty have experience flying full-sized aeroplanes and gliders. When sitting in the cockpit, a right-hand stick movement produces a turn to starboard, whichever direction the flight is going. The pilot moves with the aircraft. But when the pilot is on the ground and the model glider is flying with the nose pointing sometimes away and sometimes towards this standpoint, it can be quite confusing. It has been found that practice with a radio controlled car or boat helps with this. The situation is very similar. If the vehicle is moving away from the driver, steering is quite natural. Turning the car round to come back again, produces the 'reversed' effect.

This is especially alarming when approaching to make a landing, because the glider is coming towards the pilot. Many beginners turn the wrong way at crucial moments when landing.

When the glider is coming head on, and one wing goes down, remember to move the stick towards the lower wing to bring it up again. One may think of the control stick as a prop which can be moved over to hold up the drooping wing. That is, if the glider banks and veers off to the left, prop it up on that side by moving the stick over to the left.

Naturally, to make a deliberate turn to the pilot's left, which is a right turn to the glider when it is coming 'head on', the 'prop' may be pulled away from the left towards the right side.

Some trainees actually turn, or half turn, their backs to the glider when it is flying towards them, and screw their necks round to look over their shoulder. The control movements then seem more natural because the transmitter box is in line with the direction of flight, but the position is very uncomfortable. The problem gradually disappears and the correct movements come instinctively.

PATTERNS IN THE SKY

Having mastered turning and learned to deal with stalls, polish up and add precision. Imagine, before taking off, a pattern which the model is to make in the air, and concentrate on completing the pattern as accurately and safely as possible. Go on with this exercise until it can be completed correctly every time, then invent a new pattern and fly that. This is the difference between controlling a model and merely letting it wander about. A square pattern will be useful when flying a circuit before landing, or when searching over flat ground for a thermal up current. A series of 'beats' across wind and back, with 180-degree turns at each end, will be useful for slope soaring. The problem of reversed control effects, discussed above, can be mastered by deliberately positioning the model so that it is flying towards the pilot, and practising turns to left and right. All such exercises improve the pilot's judgment of model attitude, flight speed, height and distance.

'S' TURNS

Make a turn to the left, then straighten out, control the up surge with the elevator, settle down again, and then turn right by the same

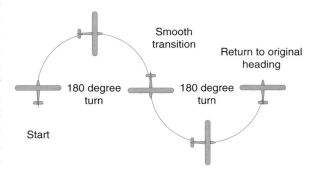

Figure 13.9 *The S turn, a useful flying exercise. S turns are used in slope soaring and to lose height in the circuit before landing.*

amount, and straighten out onto the same heading as before the first turn (Fig. 13.9). This sequence is called an 'S' turn. This manoeuvre will sometimes be needed when approaching to land, and for slope soaring. With practice, the turns become smarter and steeper, so the 'S' becomes more like a real S, always finishing up pointing the same way as at the start. Do not do S turns near the ground, however, since it is very easy to misjudge one and touch a wing tip.

FLY CIRCLES

When the pilot is confident of making a good co-ordinated turn, it is very easy to let the glider stay in the banked position, with the elevator trim slightly up, and continue right round to make a complete circle. Keep the angle of bank and airspeed constant all the way round (Fig. 13.10).

After success with this, try making three perfect circles to the left without straightening out. Keep the angle of bank, and hence the rate of turn, constant. Come out of the third circle on a chosen heading, control the upsurge with elevator and go immediately into a similar series of three turns to the right with the same angle of bank. Then straighten out and settle down again.

Ability to do this kind of exercise smoothly is the mark of rapidly increasing skill as a pilot.

When there is plenty of height, practise making continuous circles, with constant bank, in either direction. This is going to be needed a great deal for thermal soaring. A stable model, with the CG well adjusted, is capable of continuous circling flight with very little action by the pilot once the circle has been established. The angle of bank determines how much of the wing lift is being used to turn the glider. A steep angle therefore makes for a rapid rate of turn on a small radius, a shallow bank makes for a large, shallow turn.

Practise making steady circles at different angles of bank, keeping airspeed as steady as possible with the elevator (Fig. 13.11). In steep turns, the model's airspeed must be higher than in shallow turns but should not be allowed to build up until the model is diving in a spiral. In very steep turns, the stresses on the wings of the glider become very large, so do not be tempted to bank too steeply unless the wings are known to be very strong.

When turning or circling do not be misled by the feel of the wind where you are standing. The model senses only the airflow over itself. If the angle of bank is held steady and the model is not allowed to pitch nose-up and nose-down, it will

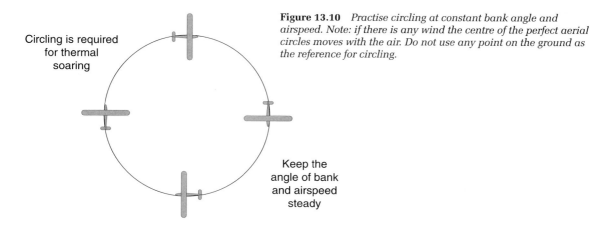

Circling is required for thermal soaring

Keep the angle of bank and airspeed steady

Figure 13.10 *Practise circling at constant bank angle and airspeed. Note: if there is any wind the centre of the perfect aerial circles moves with the air. Do not use any point on the ground as the reference for circling.*

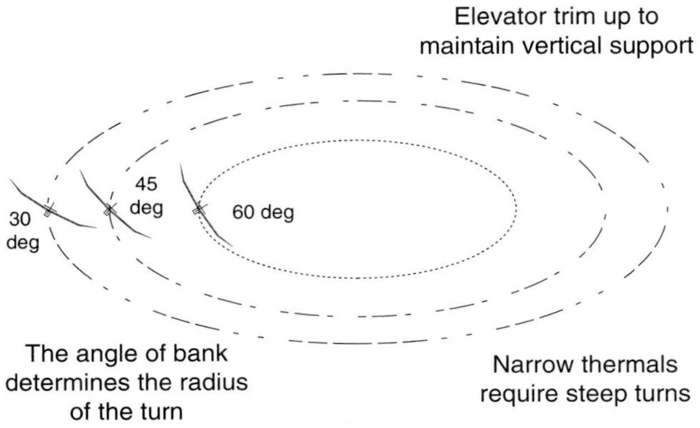

Elevator trim up to
maintain vertical support

45
deg

30
deg

60 deg

The angle of bank
determines the radius
of the turn

Narrow thermals
require steep turns

Figure 13.11 *Practise circling at different angles of bank. Note: in steep turns the loads on the structure are high. A bank angle of 60 degrees doubles the stress on the wing.*

make a perfect circle in the air, irrespective of the wind. The glider will, of course, move relative to the ground in a way which does not look circular from where the pilot stands. The general mass of air in which it is flying is moving along as a whole but this has no effect whatsoever on the air flowing over the wings and tail (see further remarks about flying in the wind, at the end of this chapter).

AEROBATICS

Even a beginner's model should be strong enough to do a few very simple aerobatics. With plenty of height under the model, ease the elevator down to gain a little extra speed, then bring the stick back smoothly, watching the model. It will pitch up into a fairly steep climb and stall severely. Neutralise controls, and bring it back to level again. Taking this to an extreme, a hammerhead stall results. In this, the model is dived to gain speed, then pulled out and made to climb very steeply. The elevator is used to keep the model going almost vertically upwards and it very soon loses all its airspeed. When the stall comes, the model pitches forward into a steep dive, almost vertically down. Pull out gently before too much speed is gained. If the climb is too near the vertical or perhaps beyond it, the model may fall over backwards instead of

forwards, but the recovery is the same. Such a backwards fall is not a true loop.

LOOPING

To loop the loop, begin with the model flying straight and level with plenty of height. Gain speed by easing the elevator down until the model is flying quite fast. Then ease the stick back smoothly (Fig. 13.12). The model will pull out of the dive, the nose will go up and up, and, if the speed at the start was enough, the glider will fly right round over the top in a loop.

The only danger in looping is that the beginner may get the model diving too fast and then pull too much up elevator, too sharply. The loop may then break the wings. Loops should not be made too tight, since this increases the stresses on the wings and, in any case, looks less graceful than a larger loop. In a good loop, the model makes a perfect circle, coming out at the same height and speed, and on the same heading, as it went into it. This is where an instructor's advice will be very helpful.

If the speed was nearly enough but not quite, the model may get up beyond the vertical position, stall upside down and topple over, instead of flying nicely all round the loop. In a correctly executed loop, there is no reversal of force or 'negative g' on the wing at the inverted stage. If

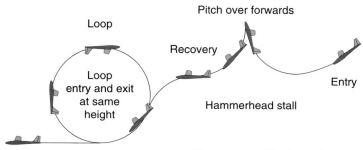

Loop

Pitch over forwards

Recovery

Loop entry and exit at same height

Hammerhead stall

Entry

Exit

Figure 13.12 *Simple aerobatics can be performed with a two-control model.*

there is dust on the floor of the fuselage, it remains there all the way round. Next time, gain a little more speed in the dive and the loop will be perfect.

If the model starts a loop with one wing low, or if the pilot allows some rudder to creep in during the manoeuvre, the glider will still loop, but will screw itself round as it does so, to emerge in a different direction from the one it was in before. Taken further and done intentionally, this can be made into a barrel roll (see below).

STALL TURN

Dive, pull up into a vertical climb and, just before the stall, give full rudder to one side (Fig. 13.13). If timed exactly right, the model will stall

and drop one wing, seeming to pivot sharply round a point in the sky. Straighten the rudder immediately to emerge flying straight the opposite way in a diving recovery. This is a stall turn. Timing is very difficult. If the rudder does not go on quite soon enough, the model simply does a hammerhead stall, but starts turning as it dives out. A genuine stall turn is quite tricky to do really well. It is possible to tail slide from a stall turn, which can damage the control surfaces of the model, so take care. The model in effect comes to a stop in the air, then tries to fly backwards for a few seconds before toppling over.

CHANDELLE

A stall turn in which the rudder is applied too soon has the glider flying round the turn

Figure 13.13 *The stall turn. A simple manoeuvre which is quite difficult to perform correctly.*

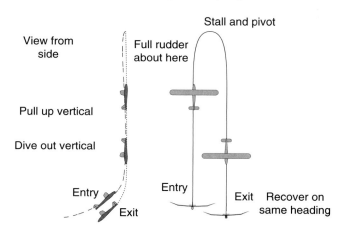

View from side

Full rudder about here

Stall and pivot

Pull up vertical

Dive out vertical

Entry

Exit

Entry

Exit Recover on same heading

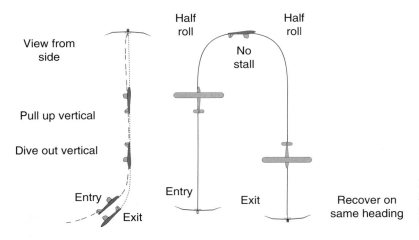

Figure 13.14 *The chandelle. The model is flown round the turn at the high point. It may roll inverted to add some interest.*

without stalling, then recovering in a dive on the opposite heading (Fig. 13.14). This is a chandelle, a very graceful manoeuvre when done deliberately but often mistaken for a stall turn by those who do not know the difference. A little more interest can be included by rotating beyond the vertical into a partly inverted position at the top, then turning back on course to dive out.

ROLLING

A roll is a manoeuvre in which the glider turns completely around its longitudinal axis as it follows a more or less straight course. Halfway through a roll the glider is upside down but still on the same heading as it started.

It is possible to perform a roll with a two-control model although it becomes much easier with ailerons. What usually happens when there are no ailerons is that the model performs a barrel roll. This is like a loop but stretched out along the direction of flight. Indeed, as mentioned above, a badly performed loop can resemble a barrel roll if the wings are not level at the start. As in a loop, in a barrel roll the model does not experience any negative g force even when it is upside-down.

To do a barrel roll intentionally requires the glider to be flying fast and straight to start with, then the rudder is applied smoothly together with a little up elevator. The model gains a little height and simultaneously banks over, then follows a spiral course through the upside down position and around until it is flying level again. Practice is needed to perfect this. Make sure there is plenty of height to recover if things go wrong.

The slow roll, as it is called, is more difficult without ailerons. The idea in this case is to roll the model around its long axis rather than flying a spiral course. At the halfway point the model is upside down, with negative g, genuinely flying inverted with the wing lifting upwards. If there is dust on the floor, it falls to the top of the fuselage.

Extra speed is needed to start, then the model is flown fast and level, the ailerons are used to begin the roll and keep it going. As the model approaches the vertical banked attitude, the elevator is eased smoothly to neutral and then down, stick forward, so that the glider is upside-down when the wings are level halfway through the roll. The ailerons continue to roll the wing round as the elevator is brought back to restore normal flight again. As before, practice is needed to get this right and two-control models are rarely capable of doing it accurately.

Another type of roll which is unlikely to happen with a beginner's model, is the flick roll. In this, while flying fairly fast, the elevator is used harshly to force the wing to stall sharply and the rudder applied at the same time ensures that one wing stalls before the other. The model actually does one, or more, very fast turns of a spin but along a horizontal line rather than descending. Recovery, as for a spin, requires a down elevator correction and straightening up with the rudder.

In any rolling manoeuvre, the model can be brought out halfway round to perform a half roll, or at any other point. Hesitation rolls involve stopping the rolling action briefly and holding it before going on. This normally requires ailerons.

Apart from the enjoyment of such spectacular flying, aerobatics are excellent practice for the pilot who needs to polish skills and become thoroughly familiar with everything the sailplane can do.

The more advanced aerobatics such as flick rolls, inverted flying, outside loops, etc., can be learned when the pilot has a stronger model with ailerons. These are best practised when slope soaring.

FLYING IN THE WIND

It is obvious that on certain days the air is too rough for model flying. For a beginner any wind above the lightest of breezes may be difficult to cope with. As the air mass moves across the land, it is generally stirred up by having to pass around and over obstructions such as trees, buildings and hills (of course for hill soaring, as explained in a later chapter, some wind is necessary and will be welcomed, but to begin with look for days with gentle breezes).

There is nearly always some wind. Unfortunately, among model fliers there is a good deal of misunderstanding of the effects of the wind on flight and a good deal of misleading advice is heard on the model flying field. This, regrettably, sometimes appears in magazine articles.

The error is sometimes reinforced by persons speaking or writing with apparent learning about **inertia**, **momentum** and **kinetic energy**. Sometimes their confused argument is muddled further by spurious, ill conceived and erroneous mathematics. It has to be most strongly emphasised that these people are themselves woefully ignorant about the terms they rely on.

Energy, momentum and inertia in flight are not measured from the ground where the pilot happens to be standing. Nor are they measured, as some writers have in all seriousness suggested, from the centre of the earth, or the sun, stars or the centre of the galaxy, or the centre of the universe.

The kinetic energy, momentum and inertia of a model, or any other aircraft which gains its support from the airflow over wings (or rotor blades), must be measured **relative to the aircraft and the air** which supports it. The glider has a certain mass, on which the gravity acts to produce its weight. Otherwise, all the forces and reactive influences felt by the model come from the air and there are no other mysterious or magical influences.

Only when it actually makes contact with the ground, when landing or crashing, do such things as momentum and kinetic energy in relation to the ground, come into effect. The diagrams accompanying this text may help to clarify the situation (Figs 13.15 and 13.16).

A wind is a mass movement of air. It is always necessary to allow for the general mass drift when flying from one point to another, or when soaring along a slope, just as a ship or boat has to allow for currents which may carry the vessel off course. Anyone steering a boat across a flowing river, for instance, has to offset the current by aiming the bow well upstream of the chosen landing spot. This offsetting of the course does not cause the boat suddenly to move sideways through the water. The water flows from bow to stern.

An aircraft carrier is steaming along at 20 knots. The air in the hangar is moving with the carrier at 20 knots. This is a mass of air moving over the surface of the earth, like a wind.

It happens that the external air is also moving. Robinson Crusoe on his island feels this as a wind. His flag is blowing out strongly. The captain of the ship is steering the carrier exactly with the wind at 20 knots. The flags on the carrier hang limply because there is no relative wind across the deck.

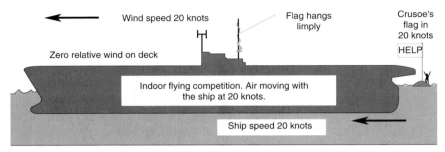

Inside the hangar there are some model fliers with their aircraft, holding a competition.
To the model fliers the air is perfectly calm because they are moving with the air relative to the sea at 20 knots. The models fly perfectly, there are no inertia, momentum or kinetic energy upsets. Turning in any direction is just the same as it would be in calm air over land.
The Captain now orders the entire lower deck to be raised up so that the model fliers are in the open.
Since there is no wind across the deck the flying continues as before in calm air.
But Crusoe is confused because he feels the wind.

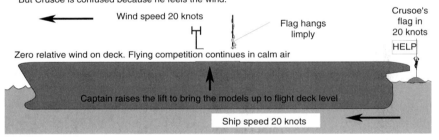

Figure 13.15 *Wind is air moving as a mass over the surface of the earth.*

If a boat sails upstream against a fast current, a watcher on the bank will see it moving slowly. But the water flows past the boat from bow to stern at the speed of the boat relative to the water. The observer sees the boat speed relative to the river bank, but not the speed through the water. If the helmsman turns the bow downstream the watcher will see it moving quickly in that direction. But the flow past the boat is just the same, from bow to stern. Pointing the boat this way or that in the flowing water, makes no difference to the water speed past the boat.

An aeroplane or glider in the air is exactly the same. Steering this way or that does not find the air suddenly coming from one side or the other, or from behind. The speed over the ground, seen by the observer on the ground, certainly does change. But the airflow over the wings and tail of an aircraft, which is what allows it to fly, does not in any way change when the flight direction is against, across or down the wind direction.

As far as the model is concerned, it is flying in exactly the same way whether the air as a whole is moving along or not. The model so to speak, does not feel the wind which moves

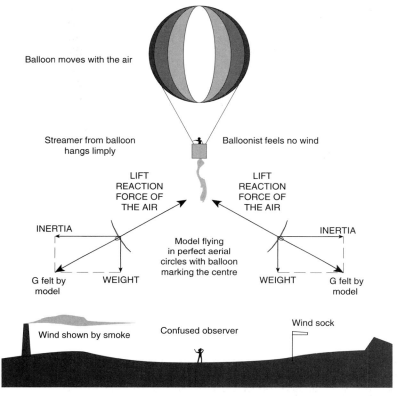

Figure 13.16 *Wind speed and direction make no difference to the forces on any aircraft in turning flight.*

across the ground, it feels only the airflow over its own surfaces.

It is therefore most definitely not true that turning in a wind causes the airspeed to change either up or down. As far as the model is concerned, turning in a mass of air which happens to be moving along is just the same as turning in a mass of air which is not moving at all, or moving in some other direction.

As mentioned above, on windy days, there are gusts and general turbulence caused by things like trees and houses. A boat in a river may strike choppy water, a model glider may run into choppy air. But the general motion of the air as a whole, the wind, does not cause changes of airspeed.

In the practical training of pilots for full-sized aviation, no mention of any supposed wind-driven variation of airspeed is made because it does not exist. No aeroplanes or gliders crash as a result. No pilot with a few hours' flying time in the cockpit has ever experienced such a thing in practice. Model fliers who remain in any doubt should go for a flight in a two-seat glider, with an instructor, and establish this for themselves.

chapter fourteen

LAUNCHING

HAND LAUNCHING

Hand launching a glider from a hill top into a slope up current, is very simple and requires nothing that will not have been learned in ordinary flying practice. It is safer to have too much airspeed rather than too little. As the model is launched, directly into the wind, a little nose-down trim is preferred so that the glider will move forward at first rather than rearing up dangerously into a stall. If there is plenty of 'lift', the model will start to gain height almost at once, even if it is being flown a little faster than normal. More is said about slope soaring in the next chapter.

BUNGEE LAUNCHING

An instructor will teach the beginner how to manage towline launching. The following section is intended to amplify some of the main points and may be of help to those who wish to practise alone most of the time. For this the bungee or hi-start is the simplest launching apparatus.

Working with a bungee is not difficult providing the weather is reasonably good. The model will be capable of managing itself quite well on the line, as free-flight gliders do, without a great deal of interference from the pilot.

Launch into the breeze. Cross-wind launching is possible with a little experience but is not recommended for the beginner. Peg the end of the bungee rubber firmly with a solid tent peg driven well into the ground at the upwind end of the flying field. A 'screw-in' type of dog tether may be used to make sure of a secure fixing for the bungee. Lay out the rubber and the attached line as exactly as possible along the wind direction, so that the model will move into the breeze as it climbs. Try to avoid rough or weedy ground where the line may get trapped or restrained in any way.

Have the model ready in a position where the bungee will have to be stretched about 60–80 metres to reach it. Get all ready for flight, with transmitter and receiver switched on, before stretching the rubber. It is better to have a little too much pull on the line, rather than too little.

When arriving with the bungee stretched and pulling, held firmly, at the place where the model is waiting, transfer the grip of one hand to the ring which will go onto the towhook, pick up the model with the other hand, point it into wind and hook the ring on, transferring the hold now to the glider. This can be quite awkward but a safe procedure should be worked out. It is obviously important not to let the bungee take over and pull the glider away before the pilot is ready. Pick up the transmitter and make sure everything is comfortable. If not, release the bungee from the hook and start again.

When holding the glider up just before releasing it, the pressure of the air on the two wings should feel equal so that there is no tendency to start off with a sudden sharp veering to one side. Occasionally at this critical moment a gust of wind will unexpectedly lift one wing and tip the glider over. If this happens, do not attempt to launch but concentrate on getting the wings level again. This may mean putting the transmitter down and using both hands to control the glider.

Make sure that the transmitter aerial is well out of the way and hold the glider high enough so that the tail does not hit your head as it goes by! The glider should be pointed into wind and launched forward and slightly upward. It will take up its natural climbing attitude almost instantly. (As soon as the model has been released the hand which held it for launching will be needed on its transmitter stick if flying Mode 1. Flying Mode 2, the right hand has control of both rudder and elevator, the left hand holds the glider.)

If, immediately after letting the model go, it veers off alarmingly to one side, use some down elevator and rudder to get it straight again.

If there is a fairly stiff breeze, the model will climb very steeply from the instant of launching. Very often the breeze at ground level is less than the true wind speed, twenty or thirty metres up. The glider rises into stronger wind as it climbs. If the wings bend alarmingly, so much that they seem likely to break, use down elevator to decrease the strain, and the model will still climb to a good height.

If the bungee was not stretched enough, or if the wind is very light, the glider will not climb well. If it seems to be going up very sluggishly, not responding well to the rudder and showing signs of stalling, use down elevator to make sure there is enough flying speed. The line will probably go slack almost at once and fall off the hook. Land straight ahead, or, if enough height has been gained, make an abbreviated approach

to land. Stretching the rubber more will help, but overdoing the stretch can damage or even break it. After a very few launches the model flier will develop a feel for the required tension and make allowances for the wind strength, weight of model, condition of the rubber, etc.

The model will climb quite well without any attempt by the pilot to force it up. The elevator can be held neutral, at least to begin with. On many occasions the model will require no attention at all as it climbs. It will level out as it approaches the limit at a good height, and come off the line by itself when it is almost over the tie-down point. If it does veer off to one side as it goes up, the rudder is used to bring it straight again, with down elevator if the sideways swerve begins to go too far.

Sometimes, especially if there is a fairly stiff breeze or if the pilot is using too much up elevator, the model may begin to swing from side to side in an alarming fashion. The oscillations can increase until the model swings so far round that it comes off the line (if this happens, it is possible to save the situation and make a quick approach and landing). The natural reaction is to try to stop the lateral swinging by using the rudder. This can make things worse. The model swings about because it is at too high an angle of attack, nearing the stall. The answer is to use a little down elevator, or at least easing off the up elevator. This has an immediate effect, killing the oscillations, and the rudder control then becomes effective again.

If a particular model gives a lot of trouble on the launch, the cause may be that the towhook is mounted too far aft. Move it forward a couple of centimetres and try again.

Pulling back on the elevator in an effort to gain extra height often causes the line to come off the hook prematurely. The glider then will go into a vertical climb and 'hammerhead' stall or even loop. To begin with at least, let the glider find its own climbing attitude and it will go up well enough. If the height obtained from the launch seems poor by comparison with similar models, try moving the towhook back slightly, but be ready, then, to correct too steep a climb with some down elevator in the moments just after take-off.

If the towline does not drop off when it should, this is probably because the line is still under tension. It can be released by a slight dive, until the pennant is seen to fall. This often happens when the model enters a thermal up current as it is launched. Recognising this, an experienced pilot will immediately circle to use the thermal (see below).

Bungee launching on days with very little wind, is often disappointing. The bungee rubber loses its tension quickly and sags, the line leaving the glider at a low altitude.

HAND TOWLINE LAUNCHING

The hand towline launch is particularly useful if the wind is weak or variable in direction. The line is wound up after each launch so can be shifted quickly to be run out in a new direction. With an agile runner it will give a higher launch than a bungee in light winds or flat calms. A simple system of hand signals is used to tell the runner when to start pulling, and flying the model up on the line is very little different from using the bungee.

It is best to have, as a runner, someone with at least a basic knowledge of model gliders and flying. An experienced runner feels the line tension and increases or decreases speed as required. If the model rises into a stronger breeze, the runner may even have to stop, or run back, to decrease the load on the wings. If the model runs into a thermal, the runner can feel this as an increase in tension and may be able to indicate it by shouting or signalling.

WINCH LAUNCHING

Winch launching is preferable to the bungee on days with no wind. Winching is not more difficult than the hand towline, but some judgment is needed to match the winch speed to the model. A light model launched at full power can have its wings ripped off. Most winches now have some adjustment or switching device which allows a gentle launch and these are perfectly safe.

Experienced competition pilots with very strong models, use very powerful winches and deliberately accelerate the late stages of their launches, in order to gain excess speed which can then be used to gain even more height. Spectacular though this is, a good deal of experience, and a very robust model structure, are essential and the learner should not attempt anything of the kind.

chapter fifteen

LANDING

PLANNING THE APPROACH

A safe landing begins before the model has been launched.

Before take-off, have a good look round at the flying field and check the wind direction. The model will land into wind, so study the downwind side where it will be making the final run in to touch down. Is the approach area clear? Are there wires, trees, fence posts, a kite flying? Are other modellers operating, and have they left models, winches, tool boxes, lying about in the area you want to land on? All these things might get in the way at a vital moment.

It is dangerous to make a landing approach by flying over the heads of other people. In the upwind direction, is there an adequate extension of clear ground, in case the model floats a long way?

If the ground is irregular or sloping, as it often will be at slope soaring sites, try to find a flat place, free of rocks, to land on, and if the approach has to be over rough country and steep slopes or near to trees, be prepared for rough and sinking air. This means making the approach with extra airspeed and a steeper glide, so the approach pattern will necessarily be abbreviated.

In some difficult sites it may be necessary to land the model on the face of the hill itself. This requires a good deal of practice and an instructor is really very necessary. The best position to stand when making the approach is near the middle of the largest, flattest and smoothest clear area that can be found, with the idea in mind that the glider will come to rest quite close without actually hitting the pilot, his instructor, or anyone else. The last thing the novice needs to consider is pulling off an exact spot landing. It is far better to make a safe touchdown in a clear area somewhere, even if it means having to walk some way, than to crash the model heavily right onto the handkerchief that someone has put down as a marker. The primary concern is always to land without damage. More accurate landings, required in competitions, will come with practice.

THE SQUARE APPROACH

Knowing the general area where the landing will be, the pilot can work out a good approach pattern. The square approach, which is the safest, begins with the glider flying downwind and still at a good height above the ground, along a line parallel to the intended landing run and about opposite to the place where the pilot is standing (Fig. 15.1). It is a mistake to bring the glider too close at this stage. This can lead to

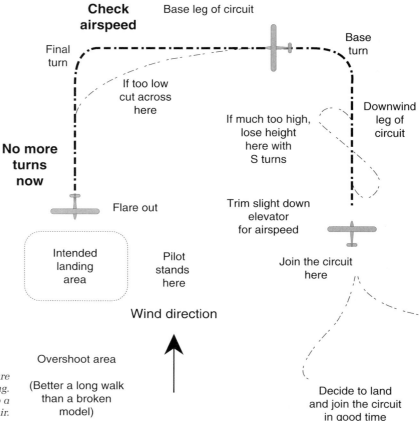

Check airspeed

Base leg of circuit

Base turn

Final turn

If too low cut across here

No more turns now

If much too high, lose height here with S turns

Downwind leg of circuit

Flare out

Trim slight down elevator for airspeed

Intended landing area

Pilot stands here

Join the circuit here

Wind direction

Overshoot area

(Better a long walk than a broken model)

Decide to land and join the circuit in good time

Figure 15.1 *The basic square circuit and approach to landing. Be ready to adapt this pattern to a particular site and changing air.*

cramping the approach, requiring steep turns at the last moment with a lack of time to judge heights and make adjustments. If there is no wind, or very little, the last stages of the circuit can be well spread out horizontally, since the glider will fly a long way forward in a gentle breeze.

Even before the launch, the circuit joining area, where the approach proper will begin, should be clear. Whatever is to be done during the main part of the flight, the glider should always be in a position to reach this predetermined point and height. If the flight does not go well, be ready to head for the circuit area before all the necessary height is lost.

The general turbulence arising from obstruc-

tions around the flying field on windy days can strike the model from any direction at any time and the model may quickly be thrown into a bad attitude needing prompt action to recover. Since the turbulence is worst near the ground, the upset is most likely to come at the time when there is little height for recovery. The glider's controls require air to flow over them swiftly to enable quick response. From the start of the circuit **trim the glider to a slightly more nose-down** attitude by moving the trim slide switch slightly forward, so that there is some extra airspeed in reserve.

The model is then flown along the downwind leg of the square pattern, and watched carefully. If it is losing height more rapidly than expected, the crosswind turn may have to be done sooner than planned so that there is enough height left to do a good base leg.

If there is some wind, the wind speed on this leg of the circuit will be added to the glider's airspeed to give a high ground speed. Do not be tempted to trim the elevator up because of this. The airspeed is what matters and this is judged, as always, by the attitude of the model, nose up or down, not the ground speed (see again the remarks about flying in wind). But the rapid progress across the ground may mean the turn onto the crosswind leg will have to be done sooner than expected. Otherwise the glider might be carried too far away to get back. If, on the other hand, the model is clearly much too high on the downwind leg, an S turn may be useful. The model is turned round to fly upwind for some way, losing height, and then turned downwind again to rejoin the approach pattern at a lower level. All such big adjustments of height are best done on the downwind leg, rather than trying to compensate for bad mistakes later in the circuit.

THE BASE LEG

The crosswind or base leg of the approach is started when the model is turned to glide across the approach area. This leg continues until the glider is in line with the intended landing place with enough height to perform one more turn and make a straight, safe glide in to touchdown. When on the base leg, as usual the airspeed should be judged by watching the angle of the fuselage to the horizontal. The usual error is to fly too slowly, so, again, the slight down elevator trim must be retained. Extra airspeed at this stage gives the pilot plenty of control.

Remember that the wind creates a current tending to drift the glider away, like a boat heading across a river. To get to the chosen spot it is necessary to steer somewhat upwind to offset the drift. The model, on a breezy day, will appear to crab slightly sideways although this does not mean slipping or skidding relative to the air.

The air is not constant. An approach which seems perfect at one moment may be upset by gusts of wind, areas of sink or up current, etc., so the pilot monitors progress all the time and adjusts the pattern accordingly. Do not become locked rigidly into a set frame. The base leg may be biased inwards to bring the model closer. If, instead, there seems to be too much height, the base leg may be slanted away. If there has been a bad misjudgment S turns may be done on the base leg although there is an element of risk in this. Do not let the model turn so that it is flying away from the landing area, and do not attempt to turn when near the ground.

FINAL TURN

The final turn is made to bring the glider into line with the landing place, facing as exactly as possible straight into wind. It is now more important than ever not to let the airspeed drop and to keep the model flying straight. These two requirements go together. If the model loses airspeed, control of direction also is weakened and a gust can cause trouble. One of the most common errors is to let the model rear up after completing the final turn, losing speed. One wing goes down and the model is suddenly veering off to one side or the other, stalling or almost stalling, and the result is often a damaged glider. As before, down elevator trim is required to maintain control but remember that in a good turn, the elevator is up slightly. Don't forget to bring it back to normal nose-down trim as the bank comes off the final turn.

Since it will now be flying towards the pilot, this is where the apparent reversed turning effect mentioned above, becomes critical. Prop up the wing that goes down, by moving the stick that way!

If the breeze is fairly strong the slowing down of the wind by ground friction is quite marked.

This is called the **wind gradient**. As the model glides down into wind to land it enters this wind gradient region and if the airspeed is too slow it will stall and drop heavily for the last few metres. Some elevator down trim was added right at the start of the circuit and this was one of the reasons. To get safely down through the wind gradient a little extra airspeed is needed.

OVERSHOOTING AND UNDERSHOOTING

If the model is high, overshooting, it will float over the intended landing place still fairly high. This is not a bad fault providing the landing field is big enough. It is a mistake to try to correct things at the last moment by doing steep S turns low down, which usually leads to a cartwheel. Let the model continue straight and level, with adequate airspeed as usual, to touchdown safely some distance ahead. In the last stages of the approach it is difficult to save the situation if the earlier planning or judgment on the downwind leg was badly wrong, but a long overshoot in a straight line into a clear area, is far better than a crashed model.

When flying at a hill siter, an overshot landing is likely to take the glider out into the slope up current again. In this case, regain a little height by soaring, settle down, then plan a new circuit, remembering what has been learned about height for the final turn.

If too low, undershooting, it is most important not to try to 'stretch' the glide by using up elevator. This almost always causes a stall, loss of directional control and at best, a heavy landing. Keep the airspeed up, retaining the down trim already established or even diving slightly to **increase the ground speed**. The glider will actually make more distance over the ground into the wind if the speed is high. The undershooting model may be brought closer by trimming more nose-down. It then **penetrates** against the wind and will float just above the ground for some distance when it is flared for

the actual touch down. An apparently undershot landing with ample airspeed, often turns out to be just right after all.

FLARING OUT

The glider should be flown straight into wind with adequate airspeed until it arrives a few centimetres above the ground, at which point the stick may be eased back very gradually to let the model flare, floating on until it brushes the grass and skids gently to a stop, still straight into wind with the wings level. Of course, no-one achieves such a perfect landing every time.

To touchdown slightly too fast is much better than stalling from a metre or two up. The glider may bounce into the air again and another landing will have to be made. At such a moment, it is easy to do the wrong thing in an effort to recover. If the glider is correctly trimmed, it should not need much action by the pilot after a gentle touch and will glide on for some way and arrive a second time, lightly. If, however, the nose is thrown up by a heavier bounce, a stall is possible, so the pilot should prevent this with a touch of down elevator. Too much will cause a dive and another, harder bounce. All that is required is to return the glider to its normal slightly nose-down glide, to let it fly on until it is ready for a correct flare out.

GROUND LOOPING

A more dangerous kind of landing is one where the model is flying too fast to land properly and also has one wing low, so at the first contact it not only bounces but drags a wing on the ground. This swings the whole model into a ground loop. It may, with luck, merely skid along sideways and come to rest without harm. Often, however, the higher wing, moving faster into the air, will lift the model up and over onto its back. It may still survive undamaged but obviously the risk of breaking something is great.

Competition pilots anxious to score points by landing exactly on the designated spot, will sometimes ground loop a model deliberately in order to slow it down after a fast touchdown. They may score more a win this way, but there is a risk of breaking something. A well-judged landing should require no such desperate measure.

A CHECK LIST

The evening before flight
1. Model in good order, repairs completed
2. Radio working, controls connected right way round
3. Check wiring, leads, switches for possible breakages
4. Place batteries on charge overnight

Before leaving home
1. Batteries charged, radio working correctly
2. Model, wings, tail, fuselage, wing joiner, rubber bands, hatch cover, all requirements safely packed
3. Transmitter with aerial, pennant, frequency key
4. Launching apparatus, bungee, stake, hammer, packed
5. Tool and field kit checked, packed
6. Check all switches off and secure
7. Hat, sunglasses, barrier cream, food, clothing

Arrived at the site
1. Assemble model, check for damage in transit
2. Observe weather, wind direction, lay out launching line
3. Check frequencies in use, wait for clearance

4. Check radio range on ground, controls working correctly
5. Study weather, circuit area, approach area, plan landing
6. Check with instructor, safety officer, fly if all well

After each flight
1. Switch off transmitter and receiver, clear frequency board
2. Discuss results with instructor
3. Check model for damage, adjust trims if required
4. Confirm radio and battery safe for further flying
5. Repeat drills and landing planning, fly again

At day's end
1. Transmitter and receiver off, clear frequency board
2. Thank instructor and other helpers
3. Check model for damage, pack safely
4. Pack launching gear, bungee, stake, hammer etc.
5. Pack transmitter, tool kit, etc and aerial
6. Remove any litter. Take care on the journey home.

chapter sixteen

SOARING

HOW SOARING IS POSSIBLE

In order to make a long flight the glider pilot must find air which is going up at least as rapidly as the glider is descending. If someone walks slowly down an escalator which is going up, although the person is stepping constantly down, the escalator moves up faster and so carries them higher (Fig. 16.1). If a glider flies in air which is rising faster than the rate of sink, the glider will gain height.

Another way of thinking about soaring is to imagine a small glider flying in a transparent lift or elevator going up the outside of a tall building. A certain volume of air is rising as a mass,

Slope soaring at Rushup Edge in Derbyshire. Beautiful scenery and a beautiful sailplane.

enclosed in the lift. The glider, trimmed for minimum sink, glides in this air but the air package as a whole is rising faster than the sinking speed of the glider, so someone outside the lift sees the glider rising relative to the ground. The actual rate of ascent is the speed of the lift going up, minus the sinking speed of the glider through the air contained inside the lift. If now the building and the lift are imagined out of existence and the package of air is thought of simply as a mass of air going up 'like a lift', the way a glider can gain height in an up current becomes clear.

If a glider is flying in an up current which is rising at exactly the same rate as the glider's rate of sink, this is like someone walking down the up escalator at a speed which just matches the escalator's upward motion. The glider will stay at the same height. Pilots often refer to this situation as flying in zero sink, but the glider is still sinking through the air. The up current just happens to equal the rate of sink so there is zero gain of height.

Glider pilots commonly speak of being **in lift**, or strong or weak lift, searching for lift, etc., meaning by 'lift' in each case, an up current strong enough to carry the glider up despite its sinking speed (this use of the word 'lift' should not be confused with the lift component of the air reaction on a wing).

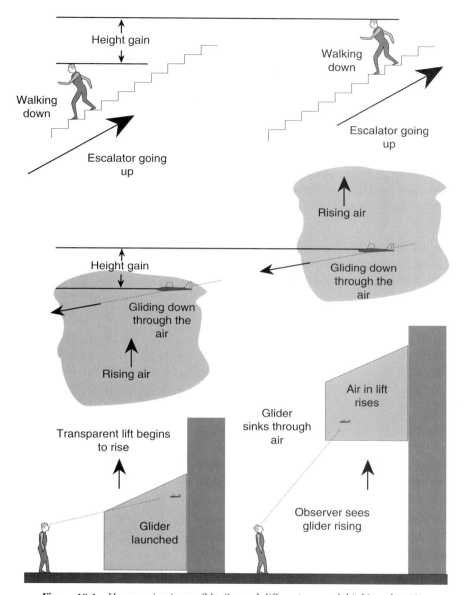

Figure 16.1 *How soaring is possible. Several different ways of thinking about it.*

Whenever there are up currents in the atmosphere, there will be corresponding down currents. As one lot of air rises, somewhere there must be air coming down. Up currents are often very powerful, but strong up currents are likely to be balanced by strong down currents. The glider pilot refers to down currents as sink. On days of weak lift, sink is also likely to be weak. The problem of soaring is finding and remaining in lift, and avoiding sink.

Two types of up current are easily recognised and commonly used for soaring. These will now be described, but do not be surprised if things sometimes happen which do not seem to fit these simple explanations. The air always has something new to teach.

SLOPE SOARING

When the wind blows against a slope, the air cannot go straight through. If the hill is long and presents a continuous barrier to the wind, the air rises over it (Fig. 16.2). All the way along the **windward face** of such a slope, there will be a region of up current or, in glider pilot's language, slope lift. A steep slope and a good breeze produce strong up currents but relatively gentle slopes and light winds can yield lift which the skilful pilot may be able to use. For model gliders to soar, the slope need not be very high. Sand dunes may be used. Large mountain slopes are also extremely productive of slope lift, perhaps too much so, for a small model can easily be lost in such country. Where the ground falls away again, the air also will go down, so on the lee-

A cumulus cloud like this marks the upper part of a strong thermal.

ward face of a hill there is always a region of **sink**.

If the hill is an isolated peak, most of the air will divide and pass round on either side. The up current on the windward side is likely to be narrow and rather weak. If the ground in front of a slope is very irregular or if the wind is blocked by other hills, the slope lift may fail.

HILL SOARING WEATHER

The slope soaring glider pilot keeps an anxious eye on the wind and weather and goes to the site which suits the expected conditions. Days with moderate breezes are best for learning. If the

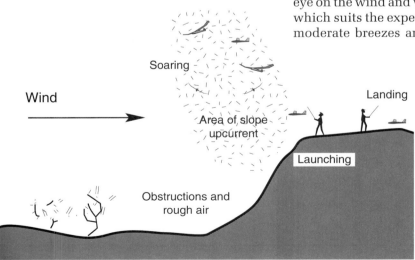

Figure 16.2 *Hill soaring.*

wind is too light the model will not stay up and if too strong it will be too rough and a slow flying model will be blown away. Later, the model flier will know when to take a heavy and fast model, and when a lightweight will be needed.

Compared with flying over flat sites, the hill soaring pilot will generally need more down elevator trim when approaching to land, because the air is generally rougher and more control is required.

KEEPING IN THE LIFT

Having launched by hand directly into wind from the top or from some little way down the front of the hill, the pilot flies the glider so that it remains above the windward slope (Fig. 16.3). The most convenient way to do this is to perform a series of **beats** or stretched out S turns. Most of the time the glider is flown straight and level, but not heading directly into the wind. Since the wind is always trying to carry the glider away to leeward, the sailplane maintains

its position over the slope by heading slightly off the breeze. From below, it then appears as if the glider is moving partly sideways, 'crabbing' along, but this does not mean the air is flowing sideways over the wings or fuselage or fin. The crabbing is simply the combination of the glider's airspeed and the wind speed, as the diagram shows.

Before long an outward turn is made. The next beat is flown on a heading which will allow the glider to continue in the lift until the pilot turns it back again and so on indefinitely, back and forth along the hill. Turning downwind at the end of the beat is a mistake, unless planning to land, since the wind will quickly carry the sailplane out of the up current. If such a mistake is made, allowing the model to be carried too far downwind, it may be possible to dive back to penetrate through the sink on the leeside and reach the front of the slope low down but fast. Otherwise the pilot has to land as safely as possible on the wrong side of the slope.

The lift area extends some way in front of the slope but is not limitless in this direction.

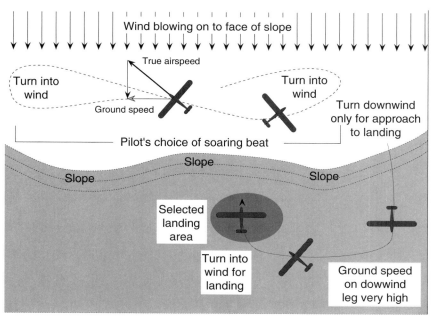

Figure 16.3 *The hill soaring beat. Turn into wind at each end of the beat and maintain position in the rising air by offsetting the drift. Turn downwind only when intending to land on the top of the hill. Perform a modified circuit and landing approach.*

Unorthodox models. Lee Murray here prepares to winch launch his Rainbow *tailless sailplane in Wisconsin.*

Upwards, the strength of the lift becomes less as the glider ascends until eventually the zero sink situation is reached. The glider can stay at this height so long as nothing changes.

Hill soaring in this way can go on as long as the wind blows against the slope with sufficient force, and as long as the pilot can see and control the glider. The life of the radio batteries becomes important, for it is easy to stay up for several hours, or to make several long flights in one afternoon.

When some experience has been gained, slope soaring will be found possible on days with quite gentle breezes. On such a day, the model never gains very much height but by careful use of the lift, the pilot can enjoy following the contours of the ground quite accurately, finding a little extra lift here and there, and using these good patches to gain height to cross the weaker zones. When turning the model, it is best to do this in lift rather than in an area of sink. In turning, the model's drag rises and the rate of sink therefore increases. If the turn is made in lift, the height is more easily maintained whereas turning in sink can bring the model down very quickly.

On a day with more wind the lift is abundant and this may be used for aerobatics, any height lost in a manoeuvre being regained immediately in the strong up current. Models with symmetrical wing sections and large ailerons are used.

THERMAL SOARING

When the sun heats the ground, currents of warm air called thermals will rise and gliders which can find and stay within these up currents will soar. A thermal may go on rising until the moisture contained in it condenses to form a **cumulus cloud**. The down currents on such a day are often strong too.

The model glider pilot may not always be able to find useable thermals, but they are almost always present once the ground has warmed a little and the pilot should never fail to look for the signs. A thermal does not have to be very hot in order to rise. Even on a cold day, if a small mass of air becomes slightly less cold, it will make a thermal. In overcast weather, if the ground is warmed slightly, there will be thermals, although they may be weak.

Thermals come in different shapes and sizes (Fig. 16.4). The whirling **dust devil** often seen in semi-arid regions is a type of thermal. Another, gentler type behaves like a rising **bubble** which develops its own internal circulation and becomes a **ring vortex**. The outer parts of the rising bubble are slowed by the surrounding air, while the inner core of the thermal is almost unchecked. The bubble turns itself inside out over and over again as the core rises, spreads out, slows down at the margins and is overtaken, then drawn in again to the centre and up through the core and so on. A ring vortex, if visible, would look somewhat like an irregular doughnut of rising air with the strongest lift going up through the 'hole' of the imaginary doughnut. Probably in many cases the rising bubble-type thermal is fed from below by a spinning dust devil type, although there may be no dust to show this.

One thermal bubble may be followed up by another and then another, making a whole chain

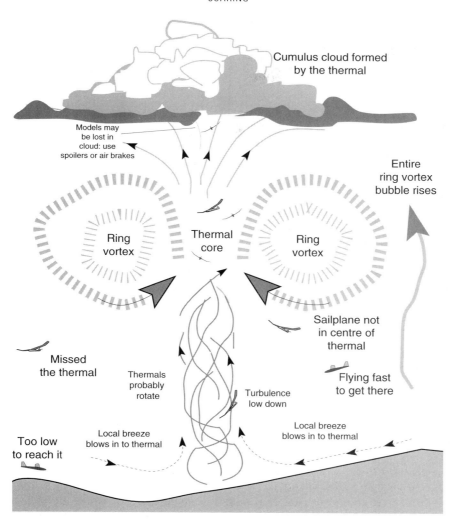

Cumulus cloud formed
by the thermal

Models may
be lost in
cloud: use
spoilers or air brakes

Entire
ring vortex
bubble rises

Ring
vortex

Thermal
core

Ring
vortex

Sailplane not
in centre of
thermal

Missed
the thermal

Thermals
probably
rotate

Turbulence
low down

Flying fast
to get there

Too low
to reach it

Local breeze
blows in to thermal

Local breeze
blows in to thermal

Figure 16.4 *Possible structure of a single thermal.*

of them in a more less vertical column or plume. A small thermal ring may be sucked in and up through a larger one and a large dust devil often winds in a number of smaller ones to itself.

Thermals also tend to expand as they rise. One which is quite narrow near the ground will be hundreds of metres across higher up. A model glider in such a thermal may quickly rise so high as to be almost out of sight, and getting it down again may be difficult. Model gliders

have occasionally been sucked into cumulus clouds and lost. Brakes or spoilers are particularly necessary to prevent such losses. The brakes are opened in good time to prevent the model going too high in a really strong thermal.

In thermal soaring the pilot's most difficult problem is to find the up current and stay in it. The beginner who runs into a thermal by accident may not recognise it. The rising air mixes with the surrounding atmosphere and the result

Design your own! Martini 5, *my own design thermal soarer with flaps and airbrakes, has been developed from the original two-control* Martini *of 1980. At the time of writing* Martini 5 *still has to prove itself!*

is a good deal of churning around. The model entering this rough air may be thrown about and the novice pilot hardly has a chance to appreciate the signs, struggling to keep the model under control. Whenever unexpected turbulence disturbs the glider, it has probably touched the edges of a thermal. It is often very difficult to tell if the glider is rising or not, but judgment comes with experience.

Some pilots looking for thermals use a geometrical search pattern, flying along a certain line for a time, then turning at right angles, then turning again to a different line to try to explore as much air as possible before having to join the circuit for landing. The idea is to avoid flying through any 'bad' air twice, always sampling a new area. If there are no other clues at all to the location of lift, such a pattern is worth using, but do not be too rigid about it.

More often than not, if the signs are looked for, there will be something to suggest where lift will be found. Look for indicators and head the model in the direction that seems appropriate, watching carefully.

Occasionally there will be some obvious sign. Soaring birds such as gulls, hawks, eagles and pelicans circling are excellent indicators. Small birds such as swallows do not do much gliding but they often chase tiny insects which are

sucked up by thermals, so a flock of swallows or swifts flying excitedly round and round probably indicate lift. If you find it, follow the example of the birds, circle round in it, trimming for minimum rate of sink.

If you see another sailplane circling it is probably in a thermal. Fly over that way unless you already have lift of your own. Do not be too proud to follow another model but try to avoid getting too close. Mid-air collisions are quite common, with one or both models usually being destroyed. If you join another circling sailplane, your circles should go round the same way as the first model, to reduce the chance of a mishap.

However, don't expect always to catch a thermal by flying underneath other circling sailplanes or birds if they are very far above. The thermal does not necessarily extend down very far. It may be a detached bubble which has risen out of reach, taking the others up but leaving only rough air in its wake. Using other gliders and birds as indicators works best if they are about the same height as your own model and not too far away.

Sometimes model fliers who have flown for some time at a particular site, will know of a few favoured 'hot spots' on the ground which seem to produce lift on most days. Find out, and try them.

Scale sailplanes. This is a model by me, to one-quarter scale, of the German Condor 3 *sailplane of 1939. It is flying here at Bordertown in Australia.*

The wind on the ground may also indicate a thermal nearby. If the wind changes direction fairly suddenly and increases in speed, it may be because the air is being drawn in to the base of a passing thermal. Such a sudden breeze may even cause flags and streamers to point to the thermal and a model that flies in the direction indicated may well find lift. Some glider enthusiasts equip themselves with light streamers on posts for this reason.

Occasionally, the wind where the pilot is standing suddenly dies away altogether. This may be accompanied by the feeling that the air is warmer. Very likely, the thermal is passing immediately overhead. If the model is near, it will probably go up.

As soon as it seems likely that the model is climbing or at least keeping its height, settle it into a steady circling pattern, watching constantly. Trim the model so that it will circle nicely with the controls held in one position. Do not worry too much if the rough air upsets the flight pattern a little but keep turning as smoothly and steadily as possible. As usual, a stable model will fly most efficiently if the pilot leaves it alone and unless the air is very rough it will continue to circle quite well once it is correctly trimmed. After two or three complete circles, if the sailplane still seems to be rising, continue circling, keeping the angle of bank constant, and climb.

Do not keep varying speed and bank, or changing direction. Working the controls too hard is bad, because the glider will respond by bouncing up and down, making it impossible to tell if it is really in a thermal or not. An apparent surge of lift which is really caused by the pilot's clumsy handling, is called a stick thermal.

CENTRING THE THERMAL

After a few circles the pilot may feel sure that the glider is not fully centred in the strongest lift. This sometimes shows up clearly. On one side of the circle, the glider rises faster than on the other side. Do not be deceived by tricky effects of perspective. Viewing from below, a false impression is easily gained, but if the glider really does seem to be off centre in the up current, make a deliberate move to locate the core. As the glider points towards where the stronger lift seems to be, straighten out for a few seconds and if the model does rise faster, start circling again. If there is no improvement, turn back to the known lift area and try again.

Just as other sailplanes may show where lift is, a glider coming down indicates an area of sink to be avoided. The main thing is to get away from this area as quickly as possible, so fly somewhere else – it hardly matters where so long as the bad air is escaped, but obviously if

Electric- and solar-powered models are popular. They are quiet and have a special fascination. This model is an electric-powered sailplane which launches itself and then glides with the propeller folded to reduce drag.

there are signs of lift somewhere within reach, head in that direction rather than merely wandering. Quite often, such sink-avoiding action takes the model into the thermal. The down current is the atmosphere's reaction to an up current, so it is not surprising that sink and lift are often close to one another. But in any case do not let the model hang about in sinking air, or it will soon be time to join the landing approach.

After a while, the pilot develops a sense of feel for thermals, and takes off every time with the expectation, rather than the mere hope, of finding something. If, on a day when other people are finding thermals, you are not, get help from an experienced instructor to find out what you are doing wrong.

GETTING HOME AGAIN

Circling and climbing in a thermal involves quite long periods of circling, so if there is any breeze the model drifts as it climbs (Fig. 16.5). Once again, remember that the movement of the glider through the air cannot be correctly judged by referring to the ground. Thermals move rela-

tive to the ground more or less with the general wind. The wind aloft is usually different from that felt on the pilot's face, too, and may be much stronger. Having circled up, the sailplane will therefore also have drifted some distance away. Keep an eye on this, and turn for home before the model gets too far off to glide back safely.

The model now must **penetrate** against the wind and get through any down currents that may lie between its position and the home base.

To straighten out on the required homeward heading will by now be easy and the 'reversed control' problem will have been dealt with. If not, still remember the mental aid, keep the model heading directly towards the pilot by moving the stick to the down going wing to bring it up again.

Once the model is established in its homecoming glide, the pilot must watch it carefully. The difficulty is to tell if the model is making sufficient progress over the ground or not. With the sailplane pointing directly at the pilot in a steady glide, if the model is clearly rising in the field of vision, it is going to get home with height to spare and will eventually arrive overhead.

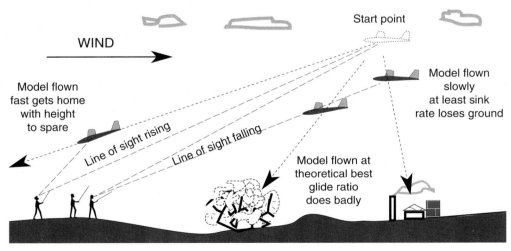

Figure 16.5 *Returning to base after a thermal climb. The sailplane which is flown fast has the best chance of getting home against the wind. Flying slowly is the wrong technique.*

The model itself will usually be losing height, but from the pilot's position, if it is going to get back, it will appear at higher and higher angles against the background.

If, on the other hand, the glider seems to be dropping down steadily, it will not get home. This requires action but not, perhaps, what the beginner expects. The trim for best sinking speed, which has been used while circling in the thermal, is at a slow airspeed, say 8 knots. Suppose the wind speed is 10 knots and the glider, at its minimum sink trim, is flying against this breeze at 8 knots. The glider will actually move backwards relative to the ground and land further away than it started. Of course this does not mean the glider is flying backwards through the air. It is still gliding ahead through the air, but the air as a whole is moving faster than the glider's airspeed, so from the ground the glider is seen to be getting farther and farther away.

The beginner's next reaction is to think of trimming a little faster than minimum sink, to achieve the best glide ratio. This is better but if the **best L/D airspeed** is, say, 11 knots, the glider will make very little progress against a 10 knot breeze. The trim required to get home against the wind is **always faster than the best L/D trim**. More down is required on the elevator, even though this at first seems quite strange to the beginner. In fact 20 or 25 knots airspeed might be required. This is a much faster trim than the best glide. The model will come down quite steeply, even appearing to be in a shallow dive with its nose well down, but it will make headway over the ground, which in this situation is essential.

This general argument applies to all sailplanes and all wind speeds. **To get home against the wind requires a fast trim**, even though this causes a rapid rate of descent. Despite instincts, trim further forward if the model is being drifted too far back. Continue to watch the angle. If the trim is fast enough, the model heading homeward will rise in the pilot's field of view. Although it is losing height rapidly it is making headway and will get home with some height to spare. Continue to monitor progress because there may be sink and strong gusts of wind on the way.

If the model seems to remain at the same angle, neither gaining nor losing elevation, it will just get home for an immediate landing. Speeding up a little may bring it back with more altitude.

With some lightweight models in a stiff breeze, it may not be possible to get home at all. Such models have poor penetration. When flying fast they lose height very rapidly. Even so, to fly fast is the best hope. It may not be possible to get all the way back, but trimming forward will get the model down as close to home as possible. Slowing down under these circumstances will have the model being carried away far downwind and out of sight. This is one important point where the more advanced sailplane has an advantage over the relatively slow and light beginners' models. Because they can fly fast without much increase of sinking speed, advanced models can make rapid headway against quite a stiff breeze

Hand-launched thermal soaring is very popular. This is my Monarch, *1.5 metres span, an American design.*

WAVES

Waves in the air sometimes develop when the wind blowing down the lee side of a range of hills sets up a wave-like pattern which extends downwind sometimes hundreds of kilometres (Fig. 16.6). Favourable conditions of air temperature aloft are required. Waves which form early in the morning may break up as the day goes on, to re-form, perhaps, near nightfall. Large atmospheric waves in the lee of mountain ranges have been used by full-sized sailplanes to reach 15,000 metres (50,000 feet) above sea level. Such huge lee waves are usually marked by distinctive whale-backed lenticular clouds aligned parallel to the mountain range and stacking in layers up to the stratosphere.

Model fliers also speak of 'wave' soaring when there is a patch of lift which they can use almost as if it were a wave, but which probably is a particularly persistent thermal which provides lift for some time over one place on the ground and then fades away. A true lee wave usually continues for many hours and may even go on for days at a time. The up current of a true wave is very smooth, very different from a thermal.

Model sailplanes have, on rare occasions, found small but genuine lee waves and used them somewhat in the manner of slope soaring, by keeping on the upwind side. Little waves are probably quite common but are not marked by clouds, so they are not often discovered. There is plenty of scope for exploration and investigation.

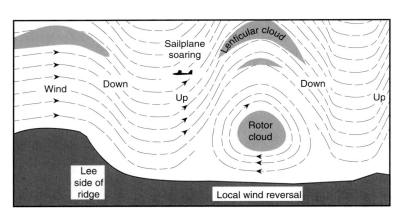

Figure 16.6 *Lee waves often form on the downwind side of slopes. Sailplanes may use them to soar to great heights.*

chapter seventeen

WHAT NEXT?

Once the basics are mastered there are many exciting things to be done. Contest flying is one way of improving one's skills. Something is learned on almost every flight and one finds oneself launching and flying in a wide variety of conditions, sometimes on days when otherwise the model would not even be assembled.

THERMAL SOARING CONTESTS

Thermal soaring competitions usually involve attempting a flight of a specified duration, such as six minutes, and trying to land within a marked circle. Points are lost for going either over or under the six minutes, and for missing the landing circle. Since such contests are popular, special rules have to be applied to make sure everyone has a fair chance to compete in the limited time available. The luck factor is controlled as far as it can be by grouping competitors into rounds and heats, five or six gliders (on radio channels that do not clash) all being launched within a narrow time slot to make what use they can of the air at that time. The winner of each heat scores 1000 points and the others are scaled pro-rata, so that if one entire heat strikes a bad period with no thermals, the scores are still comparable to those of the luckier groups. Several rounds are arranged during the day to try to arrange for every pilot to fly against every other, though this is not possible when two share the same radio channel.

In the International F3J thermal soaring class, models tend to be large but are launched only by 150m hand towline. In less important club competitions, winch launching is usually allowed. Pulleys are also used to enable the launches to be fast and high.

MULTI-TASK COMPETITIONS

The International F3B Championships for thermal soarers, at the time of writing, require each pilot to fly three distinct tasks: (A) duration with spot landing, (B) distance, and (C) speed. Rounds and heats are arranged, to remove the element of luck as far as possible.

The duration task in this type of competition is similar to that described above but with a more rigidly defined spot landing system.

The distance task requires the pilot to complete the greatest possible number of laps of a 150 metre course, within a time of four minutes. Twenty laps (3km) would count as a good performance but would probably be exceeded by the winner. An average flight speed of 45 km/h would be required, with a good glide ratio at that speed.

111

In the speed task, four laps of the same 150m course are flown as fast as possible. Times of around 18 to 20 seconds would be good, but the winner might do better than this. Speeds over 120 km/h are required to win.

Models for this type of contest are normally launched very fast by powerful electric winches and are loaded with ballast for the speed and distance tasks. They need to be extremely strong and aerodynamically very refined.

PYLON RACING

For pylon racing, markers are set up at the ends of a slope soaring beat, with observers and flags or some other type of signal. The pilots compete to fly a given number of laps as fast as possible against the stopwatch. In strong winds the models are flown low down and very fast. Pylon racing is still possible in light winds, becoming a more subtle test of skill and experience.

CROSS-COUNTRY FLYING

Cross-country racing is also done by slope soaring and/or thermal soaring. Where there is a suitable stretch of country, the pilots have to launch at a designated point and fly the models round one or more distant marks to complete the course without landing. Planning the route is up to the pilot, who has to walk or run, or travel by car to keep pace with the model as it is controlled round the aerial course.

It is likely that in future cross-country flying with large model sailplanes will involve sophisticated instruments with radio transmitters in the model to send information down to the pilot on the ground and possibly the GPS (global positioning sytem) for navigation.

AEROBATICS

When slope soaring, since the pilot can rely on the up current being there so long as the wind goes on blowing, a sailplane may perform almost continuous aerobatics. Height lost can be regained easily so not only the occasional loop but every kind of manoeuvre can be performed. To achieve some of these a specially designed model is needed. Those interested in this kind of flying soon find suitable designs.

BUILDING FROM PLANS

Many model fliers build only from kits and are reluctant to undertake building a model from a published plan. They miss a great deal. There are plans available for a great variety of different gliders and all are interesting to build as well as to fly. Some find their chief interest in trying out new designs and types of sailplane, and often go on eventually to become designers in their own right.

BECOME A DESIGNER

Designing a new type of sailplane is not as difficult as some people suppose. Anyone can make a start at this by taking an existing, successful model and thinking of some way to improve it. Perhaps a structural weakness has been noticed. Strengthening it without adding too much weight or complication is the beginning of a redesign. After success with this, perhaps a plain rectangular wing could be tapered, or a tail unit changed to a V layout or T tail. Perhaps a new wing tip shape would improve things. A new aerofoil section might help. This means changing the shape of the wing ribs or possibly cutting a foam core to a different shape, without altering much else. Build the model and fly it to see if it is better than the old one. Changing a little at a time, eventually an entirely new sailplane emerges. There are books on aerodynamics and articles on glider design in some of the publications listed in Appendix 1, that will help with more advanced projects.

UNORTHODOX GLIDERS

From designing or building from plans, it is a small step to trying something really different. Tailless models with no horizontal stabilisers fly quite well, when properly designed. Stability is provided chiefly by adding ballast in the nose to bring the balance point of the model well forward. The wing is often swept back and a special type of wing section with reflexed camber may be necessary. Although some enthusiasts believe the tailless model should perform better than orthodox models, their hopes do not seem to be realised in practice.

The canard layout, with the tail apparently in front of the mainplane, is also occasionally seen. The fore plane of a canard carries a fairly large proportion of the total lifting load, unlike the tailplane of an orthodox type. As with the tailless model, canards are thought to have a advantages in controllability and efficiency but this does not always appear.

SCALE SAILPLANES

Scale models of full-sized sailplanes are often built, some of these being very large. In flight they are almost indistinguishable from their larger prototypes. One-third scale models with spans about 9 metres (29 feet) have been built and flown very successfully. Special contests are held from time to time. Aerotowed launches with scale models of the appropriate glider tug aircraft, are becoming almost the norm in this area.

MOTORISED GLIDERS

Almost any glider can be fitted with an engine, either in the nose like an orthodox powered aeroplane, or on a special pylon. This enables a glider to launch itself but the extra complication, cost and noise of the engine has to be taken into account. When the engine stops, the drag of the motor and propeller tend to spoil the glide slightly. Models have been built which imitate the full-scale self-launching sailplane. In these the engine and propeller, after use, fold away entirely inside the fuselage, and the aircraft becomes a true sailplane.

ELECTRIC POWERED GLIDERS

A very interesting type of motorised sailplane is powered by an electric motor with a folding propeller. There are special contests for these. The batteries driving the motor are heavy and a special structure is needed. The motors are quite expensive. The current drain is high and the batteries run down quickly in flight. Recharging them rapidly takes special equipment. For a beginner to start with such an aircraft is not unreasonable providing there is expert advice available. Otherwise, learn to fly first with a simple glider and convert to this rather specialised type of flying when some experience has been gained with ordinary sailplanes.

PSS GLIDERS

A model which would normally be expected to have an engine will fly well as a glider. Powered models become gliders anyway, when the engine stops. Scale models of powered aeroplanes, especially jet-propelled types, are often built as gliders. Such powered scale soarers (PSS) are more likely to be seen slope soaring than flying from towline launches. They are remarkably realistic but of course make no noise. Huge models of jet airliners have been flown silently, in this way.

HAND-LAUNCHED THERMAL SOARING

A very interesting type of model flying, which has become most popular, is hand-launched thermal soaring. The idea is to launch the model with a strong, fast throw by hand from flat ground, and try to find a thermal. The height reached with the throw is perhaps twenty metres (say 60ft) though some very athletic throwers can do better. In good conditions thermals can be caught and I have been able, on occasion, to 'get away' from as little as 5 metres (15ft). A beginner's two-control model can catch thermals at this height but specialised hand-launched sailplanes are much better. They are normally limited to 1.5 metres span, are built with the utmost care to be as light as possible, and are fitted with special miniature radio gear, servo and batteries. They can thus become a little expensive but the hand-launch glider has other advantages. It is small and light, takes little room in the workshop or the car, needs no launching equipment and can soar in the weakest of weak up currents.

For older pilots who cannot throw, small bungee launches are allowed in some contests.

SCOPE FOR THE CAMERA

To install a small automatic or semi-automatic camera in a model sailplane is not difficult. Interesting 'still' photographs may be produced. One enterprising club used a series of such photographs to produce sets of table mats for sale.

Some large model sailplanes have been equipped with camcorders and have filmed their flights as if from the cockpit of a full-scale sailplane. Some very remarkable film footage, including thermal soaring, aerotows, slope soaring and aerobatics, has been taken in this way.

It is possible to fit working instruments which also may appear on such films, with authentic sound effects such a audio variometers and, naturally, the sound of the airflow.

FLYING POWERED MODELS

Learning to fly a model glider is a very good preparation for flying powered models. This, however, does not mean that gliding is only a step on the way to powered flight. The two sports are different and complementary and many people do both. The appeal and challenge of soaring is strong and some glider enthusiasts become so interested that they never want to fly with an engine at all. In some ways it is easier to fly with power than to make a successful soaring flight in a glider.

Perhaps, after a time with engines making noise, spitting out hot exhaust gases and dribbling oil, you will come back to the clean, quiet sailplane with a sense of relief!

FLYING FULL-SIZED AIRCRAFT

A survey of people employed professionally in aviation would probably show that most began their careers with model flying. Anyone who can manage a radio controlled glider in the air will find the early stages of learning in the pilot's seat easier. By building a few models, even more by having designed some, a young person will gain a very good basic knowledge of aircraft engineering and aerodynamics which will remain useful.

BARCS

In Britain the British Association of Radio Control Soarers (BARCS) is organised on a national basis, with a graded set of performance tests. Regional and national competitions are organised. BARCS has its own journal, *Soarer* (see Appendix 1). The contact address (1997) is: Brian Pettit, 36 Windmill Ave, Wokingham, Berks, RG 14 3XD, UK.

Email <brian@skyquest.demon.co.uk>

Web page http://home.clara.net/barcs/

THE LEAGUE OF SILENT FLIGHT

The League of Silent Flight (LSF) began in the USA. but is now an international organisation with branches and members in many countries. The LSF has a programme of accomplishments for model glider fliers, in five levels. Write to: League of Silent Flight, 10173 St. Joe Rd, Ft Wayne, IN 46835, USA.

Web page: http://www.silentflight.org/

INTERNET AND WEB SITES

Some useful contacts and information can be found through the Internet. Try the BARCS web page (above) which includes a list of other web pages and contacts.

INTERNET EMAIL LIST

Subscribe using soaring-request@airage.com

WHY DO IT?

Model sailplaning is more than a mere preparation for something else. It is a sport in its own right, but it is an unusually creative and constructive sport.

There are very few activities which call on so many different skills as model gliding does, especially if the pilot designs and builds models from scratch as well as flying them. The process begins with an idea sketched in rough outline. The task then is to refine it, perhaps do some arithmetic, consult reference books, and produce an entirely original design. This has to be translated into a detailed specification. Materials have to be found, methods of construction worked out. The work may take a few days, weeks or months, depending on the complexity of the aircraft. The objective in all cases is a flying machine which must not merely look beautiful and respond sensitively to control in the air but, above all, soar upwards like an eagle. The new sailplane has to be proved, flown against others, to demonstrate its qualities. The entire project is followed through from start to finish by the individual or a small group of friends, a rare experience. It is all a lot of fun!

appendix one

FURTHER READING

BOOKS

A few books are listed below which any glider flier could read with profit.

George Stringwell, *A Complete Guide to Radio Controlled Gliders* (Nexus Special Interests, UK, 1997) An introductory work with a broad scope, partly overlapping with the present text but assuming some prior knowledge.

George Stringwell, *Radio Control Thermal Soaring* (Argus Books, UK, 1988) A very comprehensive text covering all aspects of thermal soaring (now out of print).

Dave Jones, *Radio Controlled Gliding* (Argus Books, UK, 1987) A shorter book written in lively personal style, containing much valuable advice for the inexperienced, with chapters contributed by Keith Thomas, a specialist in slope soaring (now out of print).

Chas Gardiner, *Flying Scale Gliders* (Nexus Special Interests, UK, 1989) A comprehensive work about an aspect of the sport which is growing in popularity, with some emphasis on PSS models.

Cliff Charlesworth, *Scale Model Gliders* (Traplet, UK, 1996) A valuable work by one of Britain's leading experts on scale sailplanes.

Martin Simons, *Model Aircraft Aerodynamics* 3rd edition (Nexus Special Interests, UK, 1994) A text covering all aspects of model aerody-namics with minimal mathematics. The only book of its kind in English.

Martin Simons, *Model Flight* (Nexus Special Interests, UK, reissued 1998). A very simple introduction to the theory of flight as it applies to models of all types.

Alasdair Sutherland, *Basic Aeronautics for Modellers* (Traplet Publications, UK, 1995) A useful and simple introduction to basic theory.

A.G. Lennon, *R/C Model Aeroplane Design* (Chart Hobby Distributors Ltd., Littlehampton, West Sussex, UK, and Motor Books International, Osceola, Wisconsin, USA, 1986) A book for the technically minded, full of useful data with emphasis on powered models but some attention to sailplanes.

Ferdinando Galé, *Aerodynamic Design of Radioguided Sailplanes* (B2 Streamlines, PO Box 976 Olalla, WA 98359-0976, USA) A fairly advanced text requiring some mathematics.

Ferdinando Galé, *Structural Dimensioning of Radioguided Aeromodels* (B2 Streamlines, PO Box 976 Olalla, WA 98359-0976, USA) A fairly advanced text requiring some mathematics.

David Boddington, *Building and Flying Radio Controlled Model Aircraft* 3rd edition (Nexus Special Interests, UK, 1996) A most useful work covering every aspect of radio controlled powered model aeroplanes, with some reference to gliders.

MAGAZINES

There are many magazines for model fliers which contain regular columns on radio controlled gliders, kit reviews, new plans, construction articles etc. These are available from newsagents and direct subscription. Specialist R/C gliding journals are also listed.

BRITISH MAGAZINES

Radio Modeller published by Nexus Special Interests Ltd., Nexus House, Azalea Drive, Swanley, Kent BR8 8HU.

Radio Control Models and Electronics (RCM&E) published by Nexus Special Interests Ltd. (address as above).

Radio Control Model World published by Traplet Publications, Traplet House, Severn Drive, Upton-on-Severn, Worcs WR8 0JL.

AUSTRALIAN MAGAZINES

Airborne published by Ropomod Productions Pty Ltd., Unit 11, 67 Garden Drive, Tullamarine, Victoria 3043.

Radio Control Model News published by Elektronic Leisure Pty Ltd., 22 Hackett Creek Road, Three Bridges, Victoria 3797.
E-mail: rcmn@valylink.net.au

US MAGAZINES

Flying Models PO. Box 700, Newton, New Jersey NJ 07860.

Model Airplane News PO. Box 428, Mount Morris, Illinois, IL 61054.

Radio Control Modeller published by RCM Corporation, PO. Box 487, Sierra Madre Boulevard, California 91024.

Model Aviation 815 Fifteenth Street NW., Washington DC., 20005.

SPECIALIST RADIO CONTROLLED GLIDING MAGAZINES

Silent Flight published by Nexus Special Interests Ltd., Nexus House, Azalea Drive, Swanley, Kent BR8 8HU, England.

Quiet Flight International (QFI) published by Traplet Publications, Traplet House, Severn Drive, Upton on Severn, Worcs. WR8 0JL, England.

R.C. Soaring Digest by direct subscription to Judy Slates, PO Box 2108 Wylie, Texas, TX 75098-2108, USA. Full of interesting material, with American background.

Sailplane and Electric Modeller (Bi-monthly) PO Box 4267, W. Richland, WA 99353, USA.

Soarer published by BARCS (see page 114) for members. Often contains valuable articles about construction methods and design as well as competition news. Secretary Brian Pettit, 36 Windmill Ave, Wokingham, Berks RG14 3XD England.
E-mail <brian@skyquest.demon.co.uk>

Thermal Talk The F3J competition newsletter. 21 Bures Close, Stowmarket, Suffolk, IP 14 2PL, England.
E-mail Jacktermtalk@demon.co.uk

The White Sheet Quarterly from Sean Walbank, 29 The Gardens, Acreman St., Sherborne, Dorset DT9 3PD, England. A lively magazine from a leading model glider club with many interesting articles.

Soartech Occasional technical publication from Herk Stokely, 1504 Horsheshoe Circle, Virginia Beach, Virginia 23451, USA. Of special interest to designers and leading contest fliers.

GLOSSARY

Aerofoil (Airfoil) section The shape of the cross section of a wing or tail surface.

Aerotow Launching a sailplane by towing it with a large powered model aeroplane.

Ailerons Hinged control surfaces on the wing trailing edges, controlling the model in roll.

Airbrakes Surfaces deployed vertically to disturb the airflow and increase drag.

All-moving tailplane A horizontal tail surface which moves as a whole to provide an elevator.

Altitude Strictly, height above sea level. Often, merely the height of a model above the ground.

AM (Amplitude Modulation) Signals carried as variations of the amplitude of the radio wave.

Angle of attack The angle of a wing, tail, or other part of an aircraft to the flight path.

ARTF (Almost Ready to Fly) A kit requiring little work to make the glider ready for flight.

Aspect ratio The ratio of the span of a wing to its mean chord.

Ballast Mass added to a model to increase its flight speed. *See also* **Trimming ballast**.

Balsa wood A species of light wood imported mainly from Ecuador or New Guinea.

Bank The angle of a model wing tilted to left or right in order to turn.

Boundary layer The very thin layer of air closest to the skin of a wing or other part of an aircraft.

Brakes *See* **Airbrakes**.

Bungee A method of launching depending on a length of stretched rubber with attached towline, or the rubber itself.

CA *See* **Cyanoacrylate**.

Camber The general curvature of the centre line of an aerofoil section.

Centre of gravity The point at which a model balances.

CG *See* **Centre of gravity**.

Chord The distance measured across a wing or tail surface at right angles to the span.

Clark Y A famous and popular wing section, with mostly flat bottom, 3% camber.

Clevis An adjustable connector at the end of a control pushrod or cable.

Control horn The small lever near the hinge of a control surface.

Crystal A small wafer of crystal ground accurately to control the frequency of a radio.

Cyanoacrylate A very rapid setting, hard adhesive developed from acrylic acid.

Dihedral The angular setting of a wing such that the tips are higher than the root.

Doubler A piece of wood used to increase thickness and strength of some structure.

Downwind Going along in the same direction as the wind.

Drag The component of the air's reaction which acts directly in opposition to motion.

Duration contest A contest where pilots fly to a set time.

Elevator The control surface, normally part of

the tail, which controls the glider in pitch.

Epoxy resin, epoxy glue A two-part waterproof adhesive.

F3B The international class of multi-task radio controlled sailplane for championships.

F3E The international class of electrically powered radio controlled model aircraft.

F3J The international class for duration thermal soaring championships.

Fin The part of the vertical stabiliser which is fixed rigidly to the fuselage.

Flaps Hinged control surfaces which enable the camber of a wing to be changed in flight.

Flaring out Flattening the glide just before touch down on landing.

Flat-bottomed section Any wing section with a flat bottom making for easy construction. Camber and thickness vary greatly.

Flutter A rapid oscillation which may affect wing, tail or control surfaces in fast flight.

FM (Frequency Modulation) Variation of the radio frequency to carry a signal.

Foam-cored wings Wings based on cores of foamed plastic covered with veneer.

Former A crosswise frame or bulkhead in a fuselage to join the sides, top and bottom.

Free-flight Flying a model aircraft without radio or any other form of control.

Frequency The rate of oscillation, here of a radio wave.

Glide ratio The angle of glide expressed as a ratio of height lost to distance through the air.

Ground loop The glider drags a wing tip on landing and spins round or turns over.

Heat-shrink film Plastic film used for covering models, tightened by applying heat.

Hi-start American expression for **Bungee**.

Incidence The fixed angle at which a wing or tailplane is set to the fuselage.

Induced drag See **Vortex-induced drag**.

Leading edge The foremost part of a wing or tail surface.

Lift (a) The glider pilot's name for any up current used in soaring.

Lift (b) The component of the air reaction force which acts at right angles to the flight path.

Longeron A long structural member of a fuselage, providing strength and stiffness.

Minimum sink (Min sink) The least possible rate of descent of a glider when flying in still air.

Mode 1 The directional control on the right hand transmitter stick and the elevator on left stick.

Mode 2 Both the main directional control and the elevator worked by the right hand stick.

Monofilament line Nylon fishing line consisting of a single strand.

Multi-task The F3B type of gliding contest involving duration, speed and distance tasks.

Nicad Rechargeable nickel cadmium battery.

Nose ballast See **Trimming ballast**.

Overshooting Missing the intended landing point by flying beyond it.

Parasite or Parasitic drag The drag caused by all the non-lifting parts of a glider.

PCM (Pulse Code Modulation) Type of modulation applied to radio control signals. PCM will not work with PPM. *See also* PPM.

Penetration The ability of a glider to fly fast without much loss of height.

Phillips entry An outdated term referring originally to a bulging under the leading edge of a wing.

Pitch Changing of the glider's attitude in flight, by nose up or nose down motions.

Polyhedral Dihedral which increases at some point part way towards the wing tips.

PPM (Pulse Position Modulation) Type of modulation applied to radio control signals. *See also* PCM.

Profile drag The drag of a wing (or tail surface) caused by air flowing over the profile.

PSS (Powered Scale Soarer) A glider made as a scale model of a full-sized powered aircraft.

PVA glue Poly-Vinyl-Acetate glue, a commonplace timber glue, not waterproof.

Pylon race A race round a course marked by pylons.

Re-kitted Ironic. The model has been reduced to

many small pieces in a catastrophic accident.

Rib A part of a wing, shaped and set chordwise to give the wing its aerofoil section.

Ring vortex A horizontal, ring shaped vortex, probably the form taken by many thermals.

RTF (Ready to Fly) A model which is bought completely finished and ready for use.

Rudder The vertical control surface hinged to the fin, which controls the model in yaw.

Rx Abbreviation for receiver.

Sailplane Another name for a glider, especially one capable of soaring.

Semi-symmetrical section Any wing section convex on both sides but with unknown camber and thickness. A term best avoided.

Servo A small motor translating the radio's signals into mechanical motions to work controls.

Sink Air which is coming down, as opposed to **Lift** in the sense (a) above.

Slope soaring Using the up current on the windward side of a hill to soar.

Snake Colloquial term for a flexible type of pushrod.

Soaring Using up currents in order to gain height.

Span The distance from the extreme wing tip to the other tip, with the glider fully assembled.

Spar The main spanwise structural member of wing or tail surface.

Spoilers Hinged surfaces which spoil the airflow over a wing when raised, similar to airbrakes.

Spot landing A landing where the model comes to a standstill within 1 metre of a marked spot.

Stabiliser (Stab) The horizontal surface of a normal tail unit, or tailplane.

Stall The breakdown of airflow over a wing or other surface, caused by large angle of attack.

Stick General term for the main control levers on the transmitter.

Stick thermal The glider appears to be soaring but this is an illusion caused by the pilot.

Street *See* **Thermal street**.

Sweepback Angling the wing in plan view towards an arrowhead shape.

Sweep forward Angling the wing in plan so that the tips are ahead of the root.

Symmetrical section An aerofoil section without camber, such as a fin section.

Tailplane The horizontal tail surface, or stabiliser.

Taper The narrowing of a wing or other surface towards the tips.

Thermal An up current caused by uneven warming of the air.

Thermal street A series of thermals in a line, giving an almost continuous belt of lift.

Tip stall One wing stalls before the other, and the stalled tip goes sharply down.

Towhook The hook on the glider to which the towline is attached for launching.

Towline A length of fishing line used for launching a glider.

Trailing edge The rear edge, usually sharp, of a wing or tail surface.

Trim The setting of the controls so that the glider takes up a particular attitude in flight.

Trimming ballast Ballast, such as lead, added to the nose or tail of a glider to adjust the centre of gravity

Turbulator A deliberate irregularity, sometimes a strip of tape or a spar running along the span of a wing, intended to modify the airflow in the boundary layer (see above) and improve the performance of the aerofoil section.

Tx Abbreviation for transmitter.

Undercambered A general term for a wing which has its underside partly concave.

Undershooting Failing to reach the intended landing point.

Upwind The opposite of downwind, the direction directly against the wind.

Vortex, plural vortices Any whirling of the air, especially behind wing tips.

Vortex-induced drag The drag caused by the vortices trailing behind wing tips.

Warp An error in construction, a distortion of wing, fuselage or tail.

Wash-in An undesirable twist or warp in a wing which increases the angle of incidence at the tip. The opposite of washout, see below.

Washout A twist deliberately introduced into a wing, reducing the incidence towards the tips.

Wave Strictly, an oscillation set up by the air on the lee side of a hill.

Web Part of a spar connecting top and bottom flanges to prevent their shearing apart under load.

Wing The main supporting component of a glider.

Wing area The total projected area of a wing viewed in plan.

Wing dropping See tip stall, above.

Wing section *See* **Aerofoil**.

Wing thickness The depth of the wing from top to bottom surface, usually measured as a percentage of the chord.

Winch A launching device, usually electric motor with drum, turn-round pulley and line.

Xtal Abbreviation for crystal.

Yaw Swinging from side to side, stabilised by the vertical tail and controlled by the rudder.